For Athanasios, whose palate never ceases to dance with my food.

The heart of her husband trusts in her, and he will have no lack of gain.
—Proverbs 31:11, English Standard Version

© 2015 Ruth Bardis
All rights reserved.

Photographs copyright © 2015 Ruth Bardis
Text copyright © 2015 Ruth Bardis

Food styling by Ruth Bardis
Graphic design by Sara Ekart

All rights reserved. No part of this book may be reproduced, transmitted in any form or by any means, electronic, photocopying, or any other method, or stored in a retrieval system, without prior written permission from the publisher.

HELLENIC KANELLA

MEMORIES MADE IN A GREEK KITCHEN

Ruth Bardis

My in-laws, Australia 1968

Contents

- 1   What is in a Title?
- 3   Introducing the Nikokiroula
- 10   Beginnings
- 18   New Food Knowledge with My New Name
- 23   Merging My Story
- 26   The Greek Cuisine
- 28   My Greek Pantry
- 55   Kitchen Conversions and Recipe Notes

- 56   Whetting the Appetite
- 86   The Saucepan and the Pan
- 134   Baked Foods
- 188   Sweet Endings

- 246   Index
- 257   Acknowledgments

What is in a Title?

Developing a title for any book poses many challenges, and I mulled over several possibilities for a few years. I wanted to address so many things, but primarily I wanted to make sure that the title I chose was eye-catching to the reader and that it accurately described what the book was about. As my husband and I were driving along the winding roads on the island of Kephalonia, I kept thinking of *kanella*. Yes, *kanella*, my favorite spice and the one most used in my kitchen. Then I thought, "What does the world know of Greece? The Hellenistic Period! That's it—*Hellenic Kanella*!"

Hellenic is a word used to describe the classic or ancient Greek empire from 300 to 500 BC, the span of time between the overthrow of the Persians and the conquest of Alexander the Great. Characteristic of the classical Greek civilization, *Hellenic* was the word used to describe Greece—*Hellas* derives from *Ellas*, or "Greek." This book is centered on what my Greek culture represents as well as on the abundance of healthy produce this country has given not only to the Greeks but to the whole world. Hellenic eating: purely a delight!

Kanella, the Greek word for cinnamon, is of utmost importance in my kitchen pantry. I use it for starters, mains, and desserts, and I absolutely delight in the flavor. My childhood memories are anchored in bagsful of cinnamon sticks, quills, and powder. There is beauty in cinnamon, the spicy flavor so exquisitely intertwined between layers of bronze bark. The closer you bring it to your nose, the clearer you will sense the warmth of its fragrance. This spice enhances, elevates, and complements any dish. So, staying true to my heritage (predominately on my mother's side, from the Peloponnese), Greek meals in my kitchen are definitely intensified by the use of cinnamon.

So, as we say in Greek, *Kali Orexi* as you travel my world through *Hellenic Kanella*!

My mother and sister, Australia 1975

Introducing the Nikokiroula

My love for good food grew on me—but my love for Greek food was part of me from the beginning! I cannot recollect a time I did not delight in food, and I didn't think twice about learning to cook as I matured. I discerned that my mother was slowly instilling in me a love for good food, which came predominately from her Greek culture. Creating good food was something that I knew I would be undertaking regardless of the course my life would take.

At the end of the day, we all eat, and to survive well, we need to eat well. My first memory (from around the age of six) was my mother telling me that I needed to become a little *nikokiroula*, and this meant learning to cook and care for the home. As I heard my mother's words over and over again, I started to know my place as a young girl: "One day you will need to care for your own home and be a good housekeeper, making sure your husband is cared for and your children are healthy. You must love to care for them and not be lazy; all Greek girls know how to cook." She was a great model of this part of our culture, and she made me want to excel in homemaking.

My parents both immigrated to Australia from Greece—my father in the '50s and my mother in the late '60s. My parents recognized that having children in another country required them to be more deliberate in making sure our family maintained our Greek roots, both in language and in culture. We children attended Greek school, learning the history, language, and way of life as well as learning how to cook Greek food. There is a saying—"imaste filoxenos laos"—which is translated as "we are a hospitable race." In fact, the word *filoxenos* is defined as "love for strangers." Greeks are quick to say "Come in, share what is mine, and make yourself at home!" Greek hospitality invites guests inside, places them in the best seat at the table, and gives them no choice but to eat. If you don't eat, you offend a Greek! Out will come *mezethakia* with a small glass of wine or ouzo, bread, olive oil, feta cheese sprinkled with oregano, and a handful of olives. Before the guests realize it, they are eating a main meal and then a conclusion of fresh fruits. After much conversation, thus permitting an interval for some digestion, an array of preserved sweets or cookies and a strong Greek coffee brings to a close the time at the family table.

I saw this lived out in my childhood years. My parents' home entertained numerous guests, families, and foreigners, and the food was all prepared with joy and with a sense of normality. Money was certainly not a deterring factor, and a sharing mentality was vital. What we have, we eat together! I, too, desired to have a home where food was integral, nutrition was paramount, and hospitality was of utmost importance.

I have beautiful memories of my grandmother Angeliki residing with us for a time and joyfully making the meals she had made for her eight children in her home village in Greece. She kneaded pasta by hand, rolling out delicate, thin sheets with a rolling pin called a *plasti* the size of a thin curtain rod and cutting the lengths of dough with a small knife. She spent endless hours at a time producing pasta that would last a year. She would do the same with pasta sauces, homemade sausages, and many similar things. The art of preserving and cooking for her generation was not one of pure convenience but of surviving with whatever was available on their land. It is said that "there are times in the poorest places that riches can be born." This was true of people of that generation as they combined flour and water, and the most delicious snack we have on our Greek tables today came about: the Greek pastries! Everything was done in a rustic way—cultivated on the family farm, gathered by hand, put together by the women of the family, and baked on fire and coals. They ate the freshest organically grown produce that made healthy meals. *Yiayia* (Grandmother) would make her pie pastry and fill it with various greens from the garden, feta cheese, and olive oil. She lived to be ninety-seven years old. She was a physically strong woman who endured considerable hardships to see her family grow and survive war. I became more knowledgeable of my Greek heritage through listening to her struggles and stories of survival. Numerous recipes in this book originated from what I observed as she cooked before me.

My food recollections as a child are plentiful and the memories vivid from a very young age. It's hard to find an actual beginning to my childhood memories of food. As far back as I can remember, we ate exceptional food. There is a Greek saying indicating the importance of food:

"One is born around the family table, and one dies around the family table." One of my distinct memories is having drunk imported spring water exclusively from Greece—the famous loutraki water from the Gerania Mountains, located at the eastern part of Corinth and reaching the limits of Western Attica. This water is filtered naturally by rocks. My father insisted that this water, which included very high levels of magnesium, was exceptionally good for us. To this day, I still buy bottled spring water!

Honey was also a major part of our diet, specifically Attiki honey. This honey is aromatic and originates from bees that collect their nectar from thyme bushes in the wild mountainous regions of Greece. My parents would oblige us to eat a spoonful a day with a handful of nuts. Dad insisted this was our form of natural antibiotics!

Our school lunches consisted of homemade meals, such as the traditional Greek spinach pie, homemade sesame bars, or olive oil cookies. We would drizzle olive oil on our toast, adding a pinch of salt and plenty of oregano (yes, from the Greek mountains).

Coming home from school, we children could smell homemade bread as we dropped our school bags on the floor and ran into the kitchen to tear the bread apart and indulge. No doubt there was a big pot of something healthy cooking away on the stove. Mum would cook enough for an army. She wanted to be hospitable and ready to feed anyone who unexpectedly came by.

To complement the beauty of food, my parents used to engage us in the whole experience of food. We didn't eat in our home just to sustain our day; rather, eating was a lifestyle, a method of staying healthy and avoiding diseases and future problems that would arise from consuming overly processed and fatty foods. As children, we took adventurous drives through the streets with our parents, and whenever we found fruit trees of any sort, my parents would stop the car and unashamedly pick straight from the trees. As humiliating as it was for us as children, I now see the beauty of it—spontaneous and comfortable, eating off the tree that belonged to who knows whom. I find myself, as an adult, doing the same thing. I get excited, I begin to salivate, and I want to eat straight from the tree. Fun and fresh!

We would also go with my mother to the fresh food markets every week and fill our trolleys with fresh fruit, vegetables, legumes, fish, and meat. Our ride home was so exciting, as we would pick at a banana or with Mum's pocketknife cut into an orange.

We were educated to love our food, stay informed about exceptional produce, and value the importance and nutrition of Greek produce and its uses.

> Better is a little which is well done, than a great deal imperfectly.
> —Plato

Kephalonia, beauty both in land and sea

Beginnings

My father, Jim, was born on the island of Kephalonia, the largest of the seven Ionian Islands in western Greece (hence the name *Kephali*, meaning "head," and *Onia*, "Ionian"). It is an incredibly striking island, its beauty both in land and sea. It is an extremely lush and fertile green island, yet it has countless rocky, mountainous regions where herbs, mountain teas, and fruits, particularly prickly pears and quinces, are grown—this island is an absolute haven for great food. It is recognized for various sweets, such as its honey nougat (*mantolato*), quince pastes (*pastokidono*), sesame bars (*pasteli*), and sugarcoated roasted almonds (*mandoles*), which have an eye-catching red color on the exterior derived from seaweed.

Kephalonia also offers exceptional local products that are used in residents' daily meals. Kephalonian feta cheese (made with the milk of goats and sheep that graze at the cliff edges along the sea) and Robola wine are particularly well known. In fact, during the month of August, a "party for Robola" takes place on the island.

Fig trees are also abundant in Kephalonia. At the beginning of the fruit season, while they are still small and firm, figs are picked and made into a spoon sweet, which is preserved and eaten all year long. Ripened figs are eaten fresh or combined into various recipes during the summer months. The same method applies to many other fruits and vegetables. Kephalonian hospitality ensures that at the end of every meal, whether in the home or in a tavern, a plate of cold watermelon is offered as a gesture of gratitude!

Kephalonia is also renowned for its crystal-blue waters and sightseeing destinations like the underground cave of Drogarati, medieval castles, and monasteries. It is an island rich in history. It had been ruled by the Romans, Venetians, and Spaniards, until the French arrived in 1797 and ended the Venetian rule. In 1864, the Ionian Islands and Kephalonia were united with the rest of Greece. Due to the Venetian reign lasting three hundred years, Kephalonia has a strong Italian influence that may be seen in its cuisine, architecture, arts, literature, and music.

As one travels north along the coastline, the aroma of mint fills the air, as does the smell of freshly opened figs. There are many obvious similarities when you eat at a Greek table and at an Italian table. The abundance of tomato-based sauces, wine, and seafood are definitely staples. The family table is bountiful, the people are loud, and the stories are pleasant.

My father, his two brothers, and their parents immigrated to Australia while the brothers were still young, leaving beautiful Kephalonia behind. My grandparents were some of the first immigrants to receive grants to move to Australia. My grandfather owned a milk bar (a local general store) and worked hard to make a better life for his family. My father definitely was the adventurous one in his birth family. From a very young age, he had a palate for healthy food. He was into extreme fitness and was nicknamed "Bodybuilder Jimmy." He examined everything he ate and to this day will devote hours to ascertaining the health benefits of a myriad of things we consume. He definitely instilled this into my mother soon after they were married in September 1970. So, being true to their Greek roots, their love for good food, and their appreciation for healthy living, they set out on an adventure to educate their children and enjoy the family table filled with nutritional food.

My father

On the other hand, my mother, Paula, was raised in Kalamata in a village called Gargaliani in the Peloponnese. My mother is a depiction of Greek beauty. Her olive skin, prominent features, and long ebony hair characterized what a Greek woman looks like. She was the second youngest of eight children. The only life she knew in Greece was that of her parents tending farms and wearily trying to make ends meet to nourish, shelter, and clothe their children. They cultivated olives, which inevitably meant that all family members had to assist in any way they could on the land. She grew up in a small cement home that did not have running water or electricity. An outdoor clay oven was used to prepare meals. Meat was eaten only twice a year, during Easter and Christmas, and in small amounts. They were exceedingly poor, yet they were surprisingly healthy. They ate only what grew on their land, drank unprocessed fresh milk, and consumed much olive oil. The ladies of the family, both old and young, would arise early and start baking bread, kneading pasta, and making preserves to feed the family. It was a production line of humble poor people's food. My mother's generation was a generation of hard-working and healthy people, a generation torn through hardship but united around a family table filled with love.

My mother

My mother's family, Greece 1950s

My parents, Australia 1970

Kalamata has a great water supply, mountainous areas, and fruitful land, making selective trees and produce characteristic to the Peloponnese. Figs, prickly pears, oranges, grapes, and a variety of wild herbs and edible weeds flourish there. Pork is the main meat consumed in this region. From roasted to salted, pork is always available in the homes of the Peloponnese. A specialty dish, *gourounokefali* (roasted pig's head), is today still served and enjoyed.

Kalamata is also widely known for its production of olives and olive oil. Olive oil from this region is considered the best in the world. As one drives through the Peloponnese, olive groves fill one's eyes. The olive tree stands as ruler in the Mediterranean land; in my kitchen, without a doubt, olive oil is king! These small, round, dangling jewels get picked and then delicately cold pressed into liquid gold, kissed by the Mediterranean sun. From the tree to the drizzle on our plates, the silkiness of the oil, with its somewhat peppery and bitter undertones, is undeniable. The taste lingers pleasantly in the back of the throat, and it leads you to think about the wonders it does for your health. What other ingredient stands a chance when olive oil is around? Add a little salt, oregano, vinegar, feta cheese, olives, and some bread, and you have a party right there! I am not light-handed with it, nor do I make any apologies for the quantity I use. Olive oil makes every meal superior. From soups to stews, from dips to desserts, olive oil enhances every food it comes into contact with.

> The one exclusive sign of thorough knowledge is the power of teaching.
> -Aristotle

Far Right: My Father-in-law, Greece 1970

New Food Knowledge with My New Name

As I headed into my early teens, my eldest brother often brought home one of his friends. This friend of his was a very handsome teenager with the coolest accent. He was the most fluent Greek-speaking teenager I knew. He often came over to our house with his family, and we regularly ate together. He intrigued me from the word go for many wonderful reasons. At the time, I had no reason to think he would pursue me, but before I knew it, and as an utter surprise to me, we fell madly in love and were soon married. This amazing man is Athanasios from Elefsina, Greece (otherwise known as Eleusis). Athanasios immigrated to Australia in the late '80s when he was nearly fifteen years old. He had not experienced much else besides Greek food. Greece was not so culturally diverse at the time, so consuming only Greek food was the norm. For his mother, Christina, the art of family cooking was then and remains paramount to her Greek heritage. She often tells me, "Ruth, my daughter, I'd have to be bedridden and extremely ill to not cook; I cannot come to terms with even the thought of not cooking." Not a day will you walk into her home and find nothing ready to eat. She is Greek, which means she will feed you!

Marrying into this family enhanced my cuisine and made me enthusiastic to learn the different ways food is cooked and eaten, from the outskirts of Athens, in Elefsina (where my father-in-law was raised) to the far north of Ydrea (my mother-in-law's native village). Greece is diverse in its cooking, and each region has its own unique recipes.

My father-in-law, Anastasios, comes from a family of fishermen. He went on to become a commando in the Greek army but never let go of his love of the sea. Born in Elefsina like his three brothers and father, he would regularly be out on their boat fishing for the catch of the day. For their family, seafood far exceeds any other type of food. No matter what banquet you have laid out for my father-in-law, if there is no fish, it's just not good enough. He is passionate when he relates stories from out at sea and about preparing fish meals, which are abundant in the Greek cuisine. My father-in-law prides himself in knowing best how to select, clean, and cook fish. It's in his blood, he says. He was born into this, and it is a dishonor to contemplate that he does not know best! He taught me the tastiest recipe for octopus in wine, and his whole fish barbequed over hot coals cannot be beaten. Like every Greek father, his joy is to serve and cook for his children the best food he can find, and he enjoys welcoming anyone else to the table, knowing that there will always be extra food for friends and strangers.

My Father-in-law bottom right, Greece 1960

My mother-in-law, Christina, came from a village in northern Greece called Ydrea. She was the second-youngest daughter of a family of eight. Both her parents were born in Asia Minor (modern-day Turkey) to Greek parents. She speaks the Pontic Greek dialect as well as fluent Greek. She often engages her siblings using this language, and when referring to meals that she cooks, she always relays the name in her dialect. She too speaks proudly of her upbringing, though it was filled with much poverty. Through much poverty came about some amazing dishes that we still cook today. It's truly intriguing to hear conversations around the table directly correlating to food being so interesting as stories are shared from their histories. With Pontian origins, she opened my Greek cuisine to some fanciful dishes well known to that region. She always wears an apron tied tightly around her waist, and the first words you hear as you enter her home are, "Come, sit down and eat." She is serious when it comes to overfeeding. Her greatest delight is seeing people sitting at her dinner table and just eating. She stands close to the stove and is ready to refill your plate as soon as it empties. There is an unspoken pleasure in the eyes of my mother-in-law when I stir a pot for her, ask her questions about food, and show a willingness to acquire her methods. No doubt she views this as a demonstration of my love for her son and my willingness to make him happy as well as a way for our relationship to flourish as daughter-in-law and mother-in-law. So, from creating pastries filled with feta cheese to constructing baklava dripping in syrup, she taught me indulgence and the overfilling of a Greek plate. Her portion sizes are laughable, but her enjoyment in having company is delightful.

My mother-in-law, Greece 1960

Merging My Story

The recipes in this book are an arrangement of foods I grew up with and meals I learned from my husband's family. This book is a memoir of recipes, each rich with distinct memories. A smell in the air, the feel of a piece of produce, a sensation on my palate—all awaken various emotions that remind me of my family. I want to take you to that special place, to the joy and excitement of sharing and reflecting around a plate of food. Sure, there may be variances with other Greek cooks, but this is my story, my heritage, my Greek table. I'm Greek. The family table is of very high importance. We laugh, we cry, we share, we pray, we talk, we eat, we cook. Food is not used primarily for sustenance but rather as a means to sit together and bond. Join my world of food and finally my kitchen, where flavors are enhanced and transformed, but where all have a common denominator: my Greek heritage.

Without a doubt, ensuring precise measurements was definitely the biggest challenge in writing this book. I cooked and recooked each meal, noting exact quantities—something extremely foreign to the Greek style of cooking. I achieved precision, but not without frustrations. My mother, grandmother, mother-in-law, and other members of my family would always see, smell, taste, and feel their way to the perfect meal. Greek mothers say, "Just add a pinch. Eyeball that. Smell. Taste as you go. Observe the color and texture; then you will know if it is ready!" As you learn to cook Greek food, you won't get an exact recipe; you must practice over and over again until you can sense the desired result. The same is true with these recipes—grasp the feel of what Greek food is about, and better still, teach your palate to understand great flavors. It's all about the love and willingness to serve others in the simplest way!

This venture has been a dream of mine for many years. My initial inspiration came not because I have such a vast collection of recipes that I have adapted, created, or quirked to fit my lifestyle or even because my cookbook collection is immense; rather, it came from my passion for healthy, home-style cooking. Mealtime is a time for people to gather friends, family, loved ones, and lonely neighbors to share a pot of food made with love. So, I invite you into my Greek kitchen. Let's experience a journey of inspiration, taking simple, healthy ingredients, making them into meals, and coming together to share stories, experiences, and lives. Let's become one family around the table!

The Greek Cuisine

Greek cuisine is encompassed in what is called the Mediterranean diet. I maintain that the word *diet* is an incorrect expression, as it is not a diet but rather a lifestyle, a way of living, a way of perceiving food. There are many benefits from this style of eating that have been scientifically shown. Some evidences have revealed Mediterranean cuisine helps prolong one's lifespan and protects against various diseases and ailments. It helps with brain function and forms of arthritis, it improves eye health and bone health, it reduces dental diseases, it fights certain cancers, and the list can go on.

The Mediterranean way of eating is also largely unprocessed, abundant with fresh fruits, vegetables, herbs, spices, pulses, beans, monounsaturated fats from extra virgin olive oil, seafood, nuts, grains, and moderate consumption of wines and meats. Essentially, the majority of foods are seasoned with a lot of herbs and spices, eliminating the use of too much salt. Bread is likewise an enormous component, primarily eaten plain or dipped into extra virgin olive oil rather than butter or margarine, which are high in saturated fats.

A note to remember when using olive oil: due to olive oil's oleic acid content (monounsaturated fatty acid), the chemical structure does not change at high temperatures; therefore it is a great all-around oil, especially in contrast with seed oils.

So, the main focus of Mediterranean cuisine is the limited consumption of saturated fats, salt, and sugar, which are all linked to heart disease. Choosing healthier fats, such as extra virgin olive oil and nuts, is a great way to help kick-start and maintain a healthier life. It is true that nuts are high in fat (albeit good fats), so moderation is fundamental. Forget the grueling diets and restrictive foods; enjoy the Greek larder and what it provides, knowing that balance and good produce is vital. Remember that the Mediterranean cuisine is recognized worldwide because people buy fresh, untreated produce and get into their kitchens and cook. It all starts in the kitchen.

Thus, from the antioxidant-rich olive oil to the plethora of fresh produce, not only is eating like a Greek beneficial—it's also delightfully good for you!

My Greek Pantry

Certain flavors and ingredients are paramount to Greek cuisine. The majority are simple staples—nothing overly fancy or hard to find. When it comes to fresh produce, consistently purchase whatever is in season for optimal taste and nutrition. This will also allow for diversity in the meals you make. A balanced array of ingredients is fundamental. I love a stocked-up pantry, so here is mine! Basic nutritional information is given as a simple guide.

(Please note that I am not a physician and therefore do not propose this information to substitute any medical treatment, diagnosis, or therapy.)

OILS & VINEGARS

BALSAMIC VINEGAR
Xidi Valsamiko

Balsamic vinegar is made up of grape juice that is aged for about twelve years to create concentrated, intense vinegar. It is used sparingly, as it has an intense flavor. Always buy a reputable brand that is labeled with the terms *tradizionale/DOC* or *aceto balsamico di Modena*. Some cheaper variations use colors and caramel flavorings, which you do not want.

EXTRA VIRGIN OLIVE OIL
Eleolado

Used in all but a few dishes, extra virgin olive oil is without a doubt the most prominent pantry item in the Greek kitchen. In times past, it was used not only in food but also as an external ointment and in religious ceremonies. In ancient Greece, kings and athletes were anointed with it. A wreath of wild olive branches was presented to the gold medalists, symbolizing victory.

Extra virgin olive oil is processed without the use of chemicals and is extremely high in antioxidants. It is the oil released from the first press-

ing of the finest and best fruit through cold pressing of the olives. For an oil to be extra virgin, the acidity must be 0.8 percent per one hundred grams. If it is higher, it is not extra virgin, nor can it be labeled as that. Extra virgin olive oil can be used in place of any recipe that requires a fat, with the exception of recipes calling for a creaming method.

Extra virgin olive oil is high in monounsaturated fat, which has been shown to help with numerous ailments and diseases, such as coronary heart disease, hypertension, arthritis, diabetes, high blood pressure, and cholesterol. It also acts as an anti-inflammatory. Don't hold back—it tastes wonderful and is remarkably good for one's health!

LIGHT OLIVE OIL
Elafri Eleolado

Light olive oil refers to the sediment that has been removed via the last pressing of the olives. Consequently, this oil is light in color and is a lower-quality olive oil. The use of this oil in Greek cuisine is rare, and I would only use it as my preference for deep frying (which does not happen often in my cooking). There is quite a bit of shallow frying in Greek cuisine, and in these cases I still opt for extra virgin olive oil.

RED WINE VINEGAR AND WHITE WINE VINEGAR
Kokkino kai Aspro Xidi

Red wine vinegar and white wine vinegar are made from red and white wines. The wines are left to ferment until they become sour. They are then bottled and distributed. Wine vinegars have a lower acidity than other vinegars. They are more mellow and complex in flavor. I use these vinegars for salad dressings, soups, various pastries, and in my Greek Meatballs (page 163) to add a little moisture.

REFRIGERATED ITEMS

BUTTER
Voutiro

I'm surprised I even have butter in my refrigerator, as I scarcely use it. I have a few sticks of high-quality real butter in my fridge for a few recipes. My recommendation is that if you use butter, always get the best quality, and if you can afford it, use organic. Always remember that butter is very high in unhealthy fat; therefore, use it sparingly or, preferably, use extra virgin olive oil. The majority of recipes in this book make use of Greek extra virgin olive oil.

EGGS
Avga

I love eggs, and the uses of them in this book are endless. Always use fresh (preferably organic) eggs. Eggs labeled organic come from chickens that have been exposed to no synthetic chemicals, antibiotics, or pesticides. Always crack the egg into a small bowl before adding to food to ensure it is fresh (if it has a foul smell, throw it out).

FETA CHEESE
Tiri Feta

What is a Greek meal without a slice of feta? Undoubtedly, it is the most commonly eaten cheese in Greece. Feta is a white, soft, crumbly, creamy, sharp cheese. The word *feta* means "slice." Feta is made with whole milk from sheep and goats, with the percentage of goat's milk not exceeding 30 percent. A table cheese that is served at nearly every meal, it is also a great cheese to cook with. It holds its shape well and adds a great saltiness to any dish. Feta cheese is high in calcium, magnesium, zinc, and potassium.

FILO PASTRY
Filo Sfoliatas

Store-bought filo pastry certainly has its place in the Greek kitchen. It is very versatile and a handy product to have on hand for quick savory pies or luscious layered pastries like Baklava (page 198) or Galaktoboureko (page 192). Filo is made of flour and water and then rolled into incredibly thin sheets. Ensure that each layer is always buttered or oiled, or they will stick together.

KASSERI CHEESE
Kaseri

Kasseri is a yellow, unpasteurized sheep's-milk cheese sometimes mixed with no more than 20 percent goat's milk. It is aged for a minimum of four months and has a semihard rind, a chewy texture, and a salty flavor, making it a fair substitute for mozzarella cheese. In the Greek cuisine, it is grated over pasta, pan fried, or eaten as is with some olives and *mezethakia* (appetizer plates).

KATAIFI PASTRY
Kataifi

Kataifi pastry is a shredded pastry used predominately in a dessert called Kataifi. It consists of little rolled-up parcels that are filled with nuts and dunked in sugar syrup. In this book I showcase it in a dessert, Mastiha Pudding (page 218). It soaks up syrup very well, and it also creates a great crunch on the top. Kataifi comes packaged in the refrigerated section of international supermarkets. Place the kataifi on a flat surface and very gently separate the strands to ensure a fluffy end result with no lumpy pastry.

KEFALOTIRI CHEESE
Kefalotiri

Kefalotiri is a hard, salty cheese that is ideal for shallow frying in olive oil (an entrée called *saganaki*). A cheese made of sheep's milk and goat's milk, it is both tangy and creamy with an oily texture. Kefalotiri is also a good cheese to grate and sprinkle on pastas or use in Greek cheese pies.

MIZITHRA CHEESE
Mizithra

Mizithra is made of goat's milk that has been boiled and then curdled by adding an acid to it, like vinegar or lemon juice. It is then strained in a muslin cloth and hung to dry. It is a very hard cheese, ideal for grating. It is white and has a very crumbly, milky, and salty flavor.

YOGURT
Stragisto Yaourti

Greek yogurt is strained, resulting in a very thick consistency. Traditionally, it is made with sheep's milk, but cow's-milk yogurt has become readily available. Greek yogurt is high in protein and probiotics, which improve digestion and immunity.

FRESH SEASONAL FRUITS AND VEGETABLES

GARLIC
Skordo

Ah, garlic—the small, white, pungent ingredient huddled in wafer-thin crispy skin enhances and is distinguishable in any meal. Garlic is extremely strong, so balance is essential to prevent it from overpowering the other ingredients. It can be eaten raw, cooked, or baked. The benefits of garlic are numerous, but it is commonly known for helping control blood pressure and cholesterol.

LEMON
Lemoni

Lemons are second to none in their uses. From savory, mains to rich desserts, this tangy fruit elevates any dish. The juice can also lessen discoloration of fresh fruits exposed to air. It is a great substitute for vinegar, and it's also an excellent gargle for a sore throat. Lemons are rich in vitamin C and help treat common colds. They are high in antioxidants and are great liver cleansers. Lemons are high in potassium, copper, iron, and fiber.

ONION
Kremidi

The bulb that makes us cry when peeled back from the layers and layers of skin. Onions come in various colors, such as purple, white, yellow, and brown. All onions have a distinct taste and strength, ranging from mild to strong. They can be eaten raw, cooked, baked, and fried. In their raw form, they add a great crunch and texture. Once cooked, onions sweeten meals and are a wonderful ingredient in many recipes. Onions help fight bacteria and also help in lowering blood pressure. Brown onions are used throughout this book unless otherwise stated.

ORANGE
Portokali

From the zingy zest to the bitter white interior and the sweet, refreshing juice inside, the orange is an incredible fruit. In Greek cuisine, it is used for savory and sweet foods alike. Greek cooking often uses the whole fruit, making it a versatile ingredient. Oranges have a diversity of nutrients, boasting vitamin C (a natural antioxidant), a high fiber content, and pectin. Pectin has been proven to reduce blood cholesterol levels. Oranges are also high in vitamin A, which helps the skin and eyes.

POTATO
Patata

The versatility and the pleasantness of potatoes are amazing. I don't know of a potato dish ever tasting dreadful. Potatoes add great texture to soups and stews; they are delicious when baked, steamed, or mashed; and possibly the most enjoyable way to eat them is when they are fried in olive oil. The skins can be either eaten or removed (ensure that skins are washed thoroughly if they are consumed). There are different varieties of potatoes to select from, depending on the intended usage.

The nutritional benefits of potatoes are many. They boost energy, they are high in fiber, and they are great for heart health. In addition, they are rich in carbohydrates, vitamin C, vitamin B complex, magnesium, calcium, and zinc. They are helpful in decreasing inflammation of the digestive system and intestines.

DRIED HERBS, SPICES, AND NUTS

ALMONDS
Amigdala

Almonds, although considered by many to be nuts, are actually fruit. The almond tree bears a fruit that has a stonelike seed within. Almonds consist of an outer hull, which is a hard shell, with a seed inside. Almonds can be added to foods, eaten raw, roasted, ground, and baked. They add a great crunch and nuttiness. Almonds are very high in vitamin E, magnesium, and copper. Almonds in this book are used in numerous desserts.

BAY LEAVES
Dafni

Bay leaves are very sharp and a little bitter. They are used for stews and soups and can be used dried or fresh. Bay leaves are known to help with heartburn and digestion. They are a good source of copper, calcium, magnesium, potassium, zinc, and iron. They add an intense flavor to tomato-based sauces. I generally prefer the dried over the fresh as it imparts a stronger flavor.

CINNAMON
Kanella

This is my favorite spice! Cinnamon adds a beautiful hint of sweetness with a subtle pinch of heat. It comes from the bark of a tree, and it releases its flavor through its essential oil. In Greek cooking, it is used for both mains and desserts. Cinnamon in tea is also delicious—steep one cinnamon quill in a pot of Greek mountain tea for two to three minutes. Cinnamon has many benefits, including helping memory development and preventing tooth decay and gum disease. It also contains antioxidants, aids blood sugar levels, and helps reduce LDL cholesterol.

CLOVES
Garifalo

Cloves are an aromatic spice used in both savory and sweet foods. Although generally ground, the whole spice is sometimes added to stews and sugar syrups. Cloves help with digestion, and if you chew on a clove, it combats garlic breath. Cloves couple exceptionally well with cinnamon.

CUMIN
Kimino

Cumin is an earthy spice with some bitter undertones. In Greek cooking, it is used only in powder form and is always added to the traditional *soutzoukakia* meatballs (page 163). It is used sparingly, as the flavor is intense.

FENNEL SEEDS
Spori Marathou or Glikanisos

Fennel seeds come from the fennel plant and have a very aromatic and intense aniseed flavor. Fennel is grown all over the Mediterranean. Both the leaves and the seeds can be used to enhance meat and give freshness to various meals. Fennel seeds are a great source of fiber and antioxidants and help lower LDL cholesterol.

MAHLEPI
Mahlepi

This spice is just exquisite. It is derived from the seeds of the cherry of the species *Prunus mahaleb*. The seed is ground to a powder, resulting in a slightly bitter, somewhat almondlike flavor. Greek Easter Bread (page 206) and various other sweets cannot be perfect without this spice. Always buy small quantities to retain freshness. You do not want mahlepi that has been ground for months just sitting on a shelf.

MASTIHA
Mastiha Chiou

Mastiha is grown on the island of Chios. It is the resin from the mastic tree and forms in small crystalline drops. This resin has been known to have anti-inflammatory and antioxidant properties, and it helps with gastrointestinal problems. It can be chewed for gum health, ground for sweet and savory dishes, or made into liquor. It has a peculiar taste, somewhat like licorice.

NUTMEG
Moshokarido

Nutmeg is the very aromatic spice used in white sauce. It marries well with cinnamon and cloves and is often used in Greek sweets and main dishes. It can aid digestion and has antidepressant and antifungal properties. It is a good source of copper, potassium, and iron. When buying nutmeg, it is best to buy whole kernels, which retain their essential oils and stronger taste. Grate only as much as you need—a small amount goes a long way.

OREGANO
Rigani

Do not substitute Greek oregano with any other types. It is pungent and has a strong smell and intense taste. It is nutritious and pleasant to eat. The difference between Greek oregano and other varieties is obvious once you have gotten used to this Greek herb—it has the power to transform a meal. Oregano has a slightly bitter taste, which balances well when incorporated with olive oil and an acid like lemon juice. Oregano is very high in antioxidants and is grown in mountainous regions throughout Greece.

PAPRIKA
Paprika

Though paprika has its origins in Hungary, many Greek dishes make use of it. It is a ground spice derived from either red bell peppers or chili peppers. In this book, I use mild, sweet paprika. Traditionally, Greek food is not hot and spicy but mild and pungent. The subtle sweetness of paprika enhances dishes and aids in digestion. It is also high in vitamin C.

PISTACHIOS
Fistiki

The pistachio nut is a member of the cashew family. It has a hard exterior shell and a beautiful seed, which is the edible part of the pistachio plant. Pistachios come salted, roasted, or raw. Pistachios are a great addition to Sesame Bars (page 203), and Ekmek Mastihas (page 218).

RAISINS

Stafida

Raisins are grapes that have traditionally been dried in the sun. They add great sweetness, both in their raw and cooked forms. They are high in natural sugars and make a tasty snack free of refined sugar. It is wise to purchase organic raisins whenever possible in order to avoid pesticide residues.

WALNUTS

Karidia

Walnuts are rich in nutrients and essential fatty acids. Raw walnuts contain high levels of antioxidants. Walnuts add both crunch and flavor to many meals. Chop walnuts and enjoy them with Greek yogurt or in a piece of Baklava (page 198).

SWEETENERS

HONEY
Meli

Where can I begin with honey? The only sweetener I knew growing up was honey. From the honeycomb to the sweet, yellow drizzling of what looks like liquid gold, honey was our go-to sweet. Greeks make abundant use of honey. It has antibacterial properties and can be used to help fight common colds and sore throats. The best-known honey in the world is thyme honey. Bees feed off the thyme flowers and create an amazingly smooth honey. A natural, unfiltered, and unprocessed honey will crystallize. If this happens, simply place the jar in some hot water and allow the crystals to liquidize. Hippocrates wrote: "Honey and pollen cause warmth, clean sores and ulcers, soften hard ulcers of lips, heal carbuncles and running sores."

SPOON SWEETS
Gliko Tou Koutaliou

Spoon sweets are fruit preserves. They are served on small plates with small spoons and a glass of water. They are very sweet, and therefore one spoonful is enough to satisfy any craving. They are made with water, fruit, sugar, and lemon juice and are cooked over low heat for a long time. Some variations add some slivered almonds for crunch and a cinnamon quill for extra flavor. Spoon sweets can also be served over Greek yogurt or eaten with Greek cheeses, such as the quince variety. These sweets are meant to be savored and eaten slowly; therefore, moderation is easy for those who avoid high-calorie desserts. You won't need more than a spoonful!

VANILLA BEAN
Vanilia

I definitely prefer vanilla beans over any other form of vanilla. The bean is intense in flavor, adding beautiful black specks to food. Vanilla beans are the second most expensive spice after saffron. To seed a pod, run a paring knife lengthwise along it, splitting the vanilla bean in half. With the back of the knife, open the pod and scrape down to expose the seeds.

To make vanilla sugar, place the seeded pod into a jar with white sugar and allow the vanilla to perfume the sugar. The longer you leave the pod in the sugar, the more intense the sugar will be. Vanilla in Greek cuisine is primarily used in desserts.

CUPBOARD STAPLES

ARBORIO RICE
Rizi Karolina

Arborio rice is a short-grain—also known as medium-grain—rice. It creates a sticky, creamy, and starchy texture, which is perfect for Rice Pudding (page 223) and traditional Stuffed Tomatoes (page 153). It absorbs a lot of cooking liquid yet retains its shape. Arborio rice is best cooked al dente, just like pasta.

CANNELLINI BEANS
Fasolia

Cannellini beans are dried white beans, which are best soaked overnight and cooked slowly over low heat. One of the most authentic Greek soups, Fasolada (page 112), makes use of these beans. This bean is a favorite for vegetarian dishes and is also gluten-free.

CHICKPEAS
Revithia

Chickpeas are part of the legume family. They are filled with nutrients and are very high in protein, fiber, and iron. These beans are also known as garbanzo beans. It is best to buy them dry and soak them overnight in water. Greeks love to eat these with a generous helping of olive oil and lemon juice in a soup called Revithia (page 99).

GRAPE LEAVES
Abelofila

I have a jar of preserved grape leaves in my pantry at all times. I love Dolmadakia (page 97); therefore, I want to be able to have grape leaves on hand and ready to cook at any moment. Vine leaves are picked during summer, and unless you freeze them to have throughout the winter, these preserved ones are a great substitute. Vine leaves are high in minerals and vitamins. It's always best to soak the brined vine leaves in cold water for 30 minutes to remove excess salt.

GREEK COFFEE
Ellinikos Kafes

Greeks cannot go a day without their Greek Coffee (page 243). It is a black coffee served with a glass of water. Brewed in a pot called a *briki*, this strong coffee is traditionally served in small, white espresso cups. The sediment sinks to the bottom of the cup and is not drunk. The coffee can be served both sweetened and unsweetened. No milk is added, but a golden layer of *crema* (froth) is achieved while brewing. Greek coffee is high in antioxidants and is good for vascular health.

LENTILS
Fakes

Lentils are a pulse and are highly nutritious. They come in various colors, including green, brown, black, and orange. The best choice for Lentil Soup (page 110) is brown lentils. They plump up when they are cooked and take on flavor well. Lentils are very high in protein and iron.

LIMA BEANS
Gigantes

Lima beans are also called butter beans. The name in Greek means "giant," hence large beans. They are starchy, flat beans that compliment other flavors well. I make use of them primarily in a dish called Gigantes (page 176). They are cooked partially on the stove and then baked. Soaking the beans overnight is necessary to speed up the cooking process.

MOUNTAIN TEA
Tsai Tou Vounou

Greek mountain tea is cultivated only in Greece and is gathered from rocky slopes in mountainous regions. Its nutritional properties are numerous: it decreases inflammation, boosts immunity, helps fight coughs and colds, has antidepressant effects, and contains antioxidants. The tea

is generally dried before brewing. The flavor is enhanced by a cinnamon quill, lemon wedge, and spoonful of honey. This without a doubt is our medicinal elixir to any common cold.

OLIVES
Elies

A wonder pot of numerous types of olives has been cultivated in the Mediterranean for many years. I generally make use of Kalamata olives. Well, how can I not support the hometown of my mother! They are beautifully salted, very substantial, and provide an exciting tang when added to dishes or eaten straight from the jar. When picked directly from the tree, olives are very bitter and need to be soaked in water for days and then salted and preserved.

ORANGE BLOSSOM WATER
Anthonero

Orange blossom water comes from bitter orange blossoms. It is a sweet, florally aromatic water used primarily for desserts.

ROSE WATER
Rodonero

Rose water comes from the rose plant's essential oils and is obtained by a steam-distilling process. It has an amazing rose perfume and is used in desserts.

SEMOLINA FLOUR
Simigdali

Semolina flour is derived from high-protein durum wheat, and when used in cooking, it develops a porridge-like consistency. It is high in iron, folate, thiamine, and vitamin E, and it also strengthens the immune system and prevents infections. It is high in gluten.

SESAME SEEDS
Sousami

Sesame seeds are one of the oldest oilseed crops. Sesame seeds add a rich, nutty flavor to food. They come from a blossoming plant called

Sesamum. Sesame seeds are exceptionally beneficial, being high in iron, calcium, and antioxidants. In Greek cooking, sesame seeds are used in desserts and are sprinkled over many pies and pastries.

TOMATOES
Ntomates

Whether fresh, canned, bottled, or as a paste, tomatoes are an indispensable ingredient for a majority of Greek meals. They're the foremost ingredient in a Greek salad. Greeks love to grow their own tomatoes, so find a local Greek and befriend him or her; no doubt your new friend will share the crop!

TRAHANA
Trahanas

Trahana is made of sour milk or yogurt that is combined with flour or cracked wheat. This mixture is left to ferment and dry out in the sun and then passed through a sieve to create the small, ball-like shape. Lactic acid is produced through this fermentation, creating the naturally sour taste. There is also sweet trahana, which is made with whole milk rather than yogurt and does not have the sour intensity. Trahana is generally used as a thickener to soups and stews.

FRESH HERBS

BASIL
Vasilikos

Basil is a wonderful herb that blends perfectly with tomato. It is sweet and aromatic and can be eaten raw, cooked, and dried. It is high in vitamin C, iron, calcium, and beta-carotene.

CHAMOMILE
Hamomilo

Chamomile is a small, yellow flower that has a mellow, slightly apple-like flavor. The Greek name is formed from *hamo*, meaning "ground," and milo, meaning "apple." It is prepared by steeping in hot water and drunk as a tea. It is said to aid in sleep, indigestion, migraines, and anxiety. It's best to buy chamomile fresh, with its flower attached.

DILL
Anithos

Dill is a herb from the celery family. The flavor is very strong and aromatic, and a small amount goes a long way in cooking. It can be eaten both raw and cooked. It has a slight anise flavor. It enhances the flavors of fish, soups, and stuffed vegetables. It also is one of the few herbs that freezes well. I place whole bunches in freezer-safe bags or sealed containers so that I always have some when I don't have any fresh dill growing in the garden. Dill is a great source of vitamin A.

MINT
Diosmos

Mint is the herb that is characteristically known for its refreshing coolness on the palate. It has menthol, an essential oil that gives it that freshness. In addition to being used in various foods, mint is also boiled and drunk as a hot or cold tea. Mint spreads very quickly and can take over in the garden; therefore, it is best to plant it in pots. Mint helps with abdominal pain and digestion.

PARSLEY
Maintanos

There are two main types of parsley: curly-leaf parsley and Italian (or flat-leaf) parsley. I typically make use of the flat-leaf parsley as it is tastier and less bitter. Parsley is probably the most-used herb in Greek cuisine. It is high in vitamin K, iron, vitamin A, and folate.

ROSEMARY
Dentrolivano

The Greek name derives from the words *dentro*, meaning "tree," and *livani*, meaning "incense." Rosemary is a member of the mint family. It is quite woody and releases an intense oil, which can be used for stews and as an accompaniment to lamb and root vegetables. It can be used fresh or dried and can also be brewed into a tea. Rosemary is known to improve memory.

SAGE
Faskomilo

Sage grows in dry and stony mountainous regions in Greece. It has a strong, spicy, and sharp scent. It is commonly used as a herbal hot tea. Sage should not be boiled but rather added to boiled water to infuse it. Fresh sage enhances dishes with pork.

ALCOHOL

MASTIHA LIQUOR
Mastiha Liker

This liquor is made from the mastic gum from the island of Chios. It is sweet and delicious when added to desserts, or it can be consumed in a small liquor glass with ice. It is usually made with fermented grapes and then distilled, fermented, and flavored with the mastic resin. It has a slight anise flavor. (See more on mastiha in Dried Herbs, Spices, and Nuts, page 37)

MAVRODAPHNI
Mavrodaphni

Mavrodaphni (*mavro* means "black") is a very sweet, dark wine from the northern part of the Peloponnese. Mavrodaphni of Patras is a known brand in Greece and has exceptional quality. Mavrodaphni wine is produced entirely with Mavrodaphni grapes (a variety which comes from the Peloponnese) and has no added fillers. The purity of the wine yields an intense flavor and color. It is generally served as a dessert wine. Red wine contains polyphenols, which help cleanse arteries from damaging proteins and protects them from heart disease.

OUZO LIQUOR
Ouzo

Ouzo is the national spirit of Greece. It is colorless, unsweetened, and boasts the flavor of anise. It has a very high alcohol content, usually between 35 percent and 45 percent. It is made by distilling grapes (or occasionally other fruit) and then flavored with anise seeds or fennel. It has a distinct licorice taste. Ouzo can be served at room temperature, chilled, or on ice (when ice is added, the clear ouzo changes to an opaque milky color).

WHITE AND RED RETSINA
Retsina

Exclusive to Greece, Retsina wines are made from white and rose grapes flavored with pine tree resin. Throughout early wine making, the lack of airtight containers for fermentation resulted in wine being exposed to oxygen, which inevitably soured the wine. To fix this problem, when wine producers shipped their wine from village to village, they decided to seal their clay or pinewood casks with pine resin. This method effectively sealed the vessels, inhibiting the wine from spoiling. Retsina wines are best served chilled.

Never go to excess,
but let moderation
be your guide.
-Cicero

Kitchen Conversions and Recipe Notes

Throughout this cookbook, I use a conventional fan-forced oven.

Unless otherwise stated,
- olive oil is always extra virgin olive oil
- onions are always brown onions
- eggs are organic and medium-sized
- yogurt is always Greek yogurt
- milk is always full cream (whole milk)
- spring onion is green onion, and
- bench is kitchen counter top.

References to,
- butternut pumpkin is butternut Squash
- corn flour is cornstarch
- minced lamb is ground lamb
- minced beef is ground beef
- red capsicum is bell pepper

All measurements in this book use American cup measurements, which are slightly smaller than a metric cup.

1 cup = 237 ml
½ cup = 118 ml
⅓ cup = 79 ml
¼ cup = 59 ml
1 teaspoon = 5 ml
1 tablespoon = 15 ml

ONE

Whetting the Appetite

Anoigontas Tin Orexi

Ανοίγοντας Την Όρεξη

Stuffed Baby Peppers (GF)

Pickled Octopus (GF)

Greek Salad (GF)

Tzatziki (GF)

Homemade Greek Yogurt (GF)

Hot Cheese Dip (GF)

Skordalia (GF)

Eggplant Dip (GF)

Olives (GF)

Sesame and Fennel Seed Bread

Greek Bruschetta

Yogurt Pastry Miniature Cheese Pies

Pork, Fennel, and Orange Sausages (GF)

Cauliflower with Feta Cheese

GF denotes gluten-free recipes

Clockwise from top: Hot Cheese Dip, Tzatziki, Skordalia, Eggplant Dip

Whetting the Appetite

My homemade olives stand attractively on my kitchen counter. They are submerged in vinegar and olive oil in a charming clear jar. The jar displays the lovely colors from the various citrus rinds and rustic bay leaves that season the olives. I love how I go unintentionally to my olive jar to scoop out one shiny olive to shy away a slight craving or to silence hunger that is beginning to cause rumblings in my stomach.

I close the lid and move away, and within a few seconds, I'm looking back at the jar. Now my senses, awakened by the tastes on my tongue, immediately start asking for more. Without realizing it, I have consumed a handful of these salty morsels, and I'm left with an overly salty sensation in my mouth. I know what I need: a lovely piece of bread dipped in a shiny, glossy stream of olive oil. This will cut through the salty bite that lingers on my palate. As I dip into the oil and bite into the bread, I remember how nicely some crumbled feta pairs with a side of Greek salad.

This is only the beginning of what occurs when you start to eat Greek meze—from one small olive to a myriad of small, tasty bites, your palate just wants to try one more.

Meze are small appetizer dishes to whet one's appetite. This chapter is a combination of primarily cold foods that can be made in advance to have ready for guests. Like all Greek meals, eating is a social activity where people make noise, eat, and chatter. An integral part of these small plates are the various dips, such as tzatziki, tirokafteri, melitzanosalata, and skordalia, served with fresh, crusty bread, olive oil, mixed Greek cheeses, and a number of mixed Greek olives. Both warm and cold appetizers are served in no particular order. Whatever is ready is eaten! Served with a small glass of ouzo or Retsina wine, these dishes are small yet healthy and flavorful. Greek meze are so appetizing that you may even forget the main meal is still to come. So, eat slowly and in small quantities. There is a lot still pending. Gaze at and indulge in a plethora of Dolmadakia, Greek Salad, and many others delicacies placed in the center of the table. Pick at each plate, never forgetting to mop up the olive oil with the bread. Eating is never rushed. Taking time to enjoy the food and the company is definitely one of the highlights of our culture.

> Wishing to be friends is quick work, but friendship is a slow ripening fruit.
> -Aristotle

The combination of feta cheese and roasted peppers is amazing. We make dips with this combination, and we eat it in our Greek salad, but stuffing the small peppers with feta cheese drizzled with olive oil is definitely a notch above the rest. I first came across these when my mother-in-law would overstuff long banana peppers with various cheeses. Like all her meals, these are excessive, abundant, and always delicious! I decided to downsize a little and use bite-size peppers. They are dainty and sit beautifully on the meze table. Though these are eaten at room temperature, they can easily be enjoyed cold directly from the fridge the following day.

Stuffed Baby Peppers

Gemistes Piperies
Γεμιστές Πιπεριές

GLUTEN-FREE
MAKES: 23 PIECES
TIME: 50 MINUTES

315 g (11.1 oz.) crumbled feta cheese

2 teaspoons dried oregano, divided

1 tablespoon chopped fresh mint

680 g (23.9 oz./1.5 lb.) small peppers

2 tablespoons olive oil

Preheat the oven to 220°C (428°F).

Place the cheese, 1 teaspoon of the oregano, and the mint in a bowl. Stir to combine and set aside.

Line a baking tray with parchment paper. Make a horizontal incision through each pepper with a sharp knife, taking care not to cut the pepper fully in half. Carefully open the peppers, making sure they don't break.

Place 1½ teaspoons of the cheese mixture inside each pepper. Place on the baking tray. Drizzle the olive oil on top of the peppers and sprinkle them with the remaining 1 teaspoon of dried oregano.

Bake, uncovered, for approximately 30 minutes or until the peppers are soft and golden in color.

—

Fact: In Kephalonia, the juice of 1 lemon is drizzled onto the peppers before baking.

Make-ahead tip: Prepare the peppers a day in advance, cover them with plastic wrap, and store them in the refrigerator. Remove the plastic wrap before baking the peppers.

Octopuses dangling in the sun to dry are a spectacle of beauty and excitement. You cannot walk past them anywhere in Greece and not stop to gaze at them. The fishermen work theatrically, and the scene they set is impressive. The fishermen throw the octopuses repeatedly against the sea rocks in order to tenderize the meat. Following this, the sea creatures are flung over a wire or rope to dry in the sun. Grecian blue skies, light sea breezes, and warm sunshine paint the perfect picture of the Mediterranean as the octopuses hang at the forefront of the sea.

This recipe is an acknowledgment to my father-in-law, who taught me how to make the perfect pickled octopus and who prides himself in having passed on this recipe from his own father to me. Keep the cooking temperature low so that the octopus literally gets a little more heat than by using a poaching method. If the octopus is cooked at a high heat, it will end up rubbery and chewy.

Pickled Octopus

Htapodi Toursi
Χταπόδι Τουρσί

GLUTEN-FREE
MAKES: 4 SERVINGS
TIME: 2 HOURS

- 1 octopus (roughly 1 kg/2.2 lb./35.2 oz.), head and beak removed
- 3 cups red wine
- ½ cup olive oil
- ½ cup fresh lemon juice
- 2 teaspoons dried oregano
- 1 teaspoon salt

First, make sure you do not add salt during the cooking process—this would make the octopus tough.

Place the octopus and wine in a saucepan. Simmer the octopus, partially covered, over low heat for 1–2 hours or until tender. The cooking time may vary depending on the thickness of the tentacles. Check that the liquid has not totally evaporated after 1 hour. If it has, add 1 cup of water.

Drain the octopus and allow it to cool slightly in a bowl. Cut it into bite-size pieces. Place the oil, lemon juice, oregano, and salt into a bowl. Mix these well, and then pour the mixture over the warm octopus. Adjust the seasoning as desired.

—

Tip: As an alternative, red wine vinegar or apple cider vinegar can be substituted for wine in this recipe. The end result will be a more pickled taste.

Ubiquitously, various versions of what some may call a Greek salad exist. One thing needs to be clarified immediately: Greek salad does not contain any lettuce. It is made primarily of ripe tomatoes, cucumbers, green peppers, feta cheese, olives, onions, Greek dried oregano, and a good dose of extra virgin olive oil. Vinegar is optional, as are capers. It is a fresh, exceptionally healthy salad, and not surprisingly, it is a big part of the Mediterranean way. It is quick to prepare and consists of ingredients that are usually staples in any kitchen. Make sure not to withhold the amount of olive oil, as this is what makes this salad so divine. Have plenty of bread to mop up the juices. Always serve this salad using cold vegetables straight from the refrigerator—this definitely makes the salad more refreshing.

Greek Salad

Horiatiki Salata
Χωριάτικη Σαλάτα

GLUTEN-FREE
MAKES: 3 SERVINGS
TIME: 10 MINUTES

- 4 ripe tomatoes, each cut into quarters
- ½ large English cucumber, chopped
- ½ green bell pepper, sliced thinly
- ¼ red onion, sliced
- 100 g block of feta cheese (3.5 oz. /0.22 lb.)
- ¼ cup Kalamata olives
- ¼ cup extra virgin olive oil
- 1½ teaspoons dried oregano
- 1 tablespoon capers
- Salt, to taste

Place the cut tomatoes, cucumber, bell pepper, onion, feta cheese, and olives in a large salad bowl. The feta cheese is traditionally placed on top of the salad in one thick slice. Add the olive oil, dried oregano, and salt, and gently mix all the ingredients. Taste and adjust the seasoning if required. Add more olive oil if the salad is a little dry. Serve the salad immediately with crusty bread.

—

Tip: For a more visually attractive salad, add tomatoes of different colors, cutting them into random sizes.

Tzatziki is undeniably our national dip. This refreshing yet garlicky and pungent dip goes well with so many different foods. The flavor develops and intensifies the longer you leave it, so make it a day in advance. It will keep in the fridge for at least four days. Use the best full-cream Greek yogurt you can find. Tzatziki can be used on meat and fish, thickly smeared on some crusty bread, or made as a dip for your favorite chips or crisps. This is my grandmother Angeliki's recipe.

Tzatziki

Tzatziki
Τζατζίκι

GLUTEN-FREE
MAKES: 3 CUPS
TIME: 10 MINUTES

Place all the ingredients (ensuring the cucumber has been strained well) into a bowl and mix well. Taste and adjust the seasoning.

Serve the tzatziki drizzled with a little olive oil. Refrigerate it, and then use it as desired.

—

Suggestion: For an even thicker consistency, you can strain the yogurt in a muslin cloth or tea towel for a few hours prior to assembling the remaining ingredients. Straining reduces the quantity by half.

3 cups Greek yogurt

½ English cucumber, peeled, grated, and strained

4 garlic cloves, minced

½ teaspoon salt

1 teaspoon white or red wine vinegar

1 tablespoon olive oil

Whetting the Appetite

Homemade yogurt certainly reminds me of my parents. My father in particular makes an unhurried point of eating it with a fancy, long-handled teaspoon and a good helping of organic honey. The satisfaction is evident as he scrumptiously digs in—to him, this is like a luscious dessert.

The thought of making your own yogurt does not need to intimidate or alarm you. I can reassure you that after attempting it once, you'll grasp how stress-free and satisfying it is to make. The uses of yogurt in Greek cooking are numerous. The most common way we ate it as children was with a good helping of organic honey, nuts, and a sprinkling of cinnamon.

Homemade Yogurt

Spitiko Yiaourti
Σπιτικό Γιαούρτι

GLUTEN-FREE
MAKES: 1L (33 OZ.)
PREPARATION: 35 MINUTES
TIME: SET OVERNIGHT

1 L (33.8 fl. oz.) whole milk

¾ cup Greek yogurt (preferably sheep's yogurt)

In a saucepan, heat the milk over medium heat until it starts to boil. As soon as the milk rapidly rises to the top of the pan, remove from the heat. Submerge the saucepan in a cold-water bath and stir until the milk has started to drop in temperature. To test if it is cool enough, place your pinkie finger into the milk—if you can count to 10 comfortably without getting burned, the milk is ready. (Make sure it's not too hot, or the milk will curdle as soon as the yogurt is added.)

Remove the saucepan from the water bath. In a small bowl, combine the sheep's yogurt and 1 cup of the boiled milk. Whisk to combine well, and then add this mixture to the pot of milk. Stir the mixture quickly to combine. Pour the yogurt into a large jar and cover it with a lid.

Place the jar in a deep dish. Boil some water and pour it into the dish until it is half full. Cover the dish with a large blanket—retaining warmth is the key here. Allow the yogurt to sit overnight, or between 12 and 15 hours. It should now have cultured adequately; refrigerate it and use it as desired.

—

Suggestion: If you desire flavored yogurt, add jam, honey, or fruits to the jar, add in the yogurt, and allow it to set per the recipe.

My mother-in-law on the donkey, Greece 1960

Good habits formed at youth make all the difference.
-Aristotle

"Hot cheese dip" is the literal translation from the Greek *tiro* meaning "cheese" and *kafteri* meaning "hot." This dip shows the great combination of Greek feta cheese and red capsicums. It is both salty and spicy. The addition of the roasted almonds gives it a great crunch. Be warned: this is an addictive dip. This dip does set a little once it has been refrigerated, so don't worry if it is not very thick initially.

Hot Cheese Dip

Tiro-Kafteri
Τυροκαφτερή

GLUTEN-FREE
MAKES: 3 CUPS
TIME: 50 MINUTES

4 large roasted red capsicums (bell pepper)*

½ cup roasted almonds

4 garlic cloves, minced

¾ teaspoon red chili flakes

¼ cup olive oil

1 tablespoon balsamic vinegar

250 g (9.9 oz./0.55 lb.) feta cheese

¼ teaspoon salt

¼ teaspoon black pepper

To prepare the capsicums, place them on a baking tray and bake them, uncovered, at 200°C (392°F) until they are soft and a little charred. Allow them to cool, and then peel away the skins and the seeds. You will find that the skins peel away very easily. Alternatively, use jarred capsicums.

Place all the ingredients into a food processor and blend. If the mixture seems too thick, add a little more olive oil; if it is a little too runny, add a little more feta cheese. Taste to check the seasoning—the dip must have a salty bite to it. Cover the dip and chill it for a minimum of 2 hours before serving. Serve it with crusty bread.

—

*Store-bought roasted red capsicums can be substituted for fresh. Place them directly from the jar into the food processor and proceed with the recipe.

Skordalia is a silky potato dip with tantalizing lemon and garlic flavor. *Skordo* means "garlic" and *aliada* means "puree." This dip is characteristic to the island of Kephalonia. It is made with skill and passion using a stone mortar and pestle to create the smoothest, silkiest dip. This recipe was passed on to me from my dear seventy-nine-year-old friend Leah, who is from this island. Skordalia from Kephalonia is known as the best in Greece. The main difference between this dip and those of other regions is that Kephalonian skordalia does not use walnuts or bread but rather potatoes and garlic. The texture is smoother and thicker. It is traditionally served with salted cod.

Skordalia

Skordalia-Aliada
Σκορδαλιά-Αλιάδα

GLUTEN-FREE
MAKES: 3 CUPS
TIME: 45 MINUTES

Place the potatoes in a pot and cover them with water. Boil the potatoes until they are soft.

Drain the potatoes in a colander and add them to a blender. Add the minced garlic and puree until combined. Add the olive oil, lemon juice, and salt. Puree again until the dip is mixed well. Serve with bread or salted cod. Keep the dip refrigerated up to 5 days.

—

Mince the garlic in a mortar and pestle with ¼ teaspoon of salt to create a paste.

6 medium potatoes (russet), peeled and quartered

6 large garlic cloves, minced*

½ cup olive oil

¾ cup lemon juice

1½ teaspoons salt

Maybe this recipe has you thinking of a similar dip: baba ghanoush, the Arabic eggplant dip pureed with olive oil and spices. This dip is comparable to baba ghanoush yet different. This recipe uses eggplants, but it's enriched by various elements that are undeniably Mediterranean. Roasted eggplants, garlic, feta cheese, olives, and olive oil combine to create a delectable dip that makes one salivate. There are a number of ways you can make this using different ingredients and techniques, but I enjoy this very traditional way from the village people of Greece. It is rustic and mixed together using a knife rather than a blender. The slightly chunky consistency is what you want! Serve this delectable dip warm or cold.

Eggplant Dip

Melitzanosalata
Μελιτζανοσαλάτα

GLUTEN-FREE
MAKES: 2 CUPS
TIME: 50-60 MINUTES

1 large eggplant, roasted and peeled

1 large red capsicum (bell pepper), roasted and peeled

1 large garlic clove, minced

½ onion, finely chopped

¼ cup finely chopped flat leaf parsley

½ cup olive oil

100 g (3.5 oz./0.22 lb.) crumbled feta cheese

1 teaspoon salt

1 teaspoon black pepper

¼ cup chopped Kalamata olives

On a baking tray, place the whole eggplant and whole red capsicum. Roast the vegetables for 40 minutes at 230°C (446°F) or until they are soft.

While the eggplant is still warm, cut it in half and spoon out the flesh. Discard the skin. Roughly chop the flesh of the eggplant (do not blend—you want a rustic texture) and place it into a bowl. Remove the outer skin from the red capsicum and finely dice the flesh. (This does not need to be perfect, but you want to be able to distinguish the pieces.)

Add all remaining ingredients and gently mix. Taste to adjust the seasoning. Drizzle the dip with a little extra olive oil before serving.

Keep the dip refrigerated up to 5 days.

What is a Greek table without olives? The first thing I learned as I was growing up was that cutlery, bread, cheese, and olives all adorn a table. One cannot be without these, and for good reason. Olives whet the appetite in preparation for the main meal. Marinating is simple, and flavors can be endless—you simply cannot go wrong. The only thing that needs to be considered is the ratio of vinegar to olive oil (I recommend filling the jar three-quarters full of vinegar and one-quarter full of olive oil). The longer the olives are left to marinate, the better. Do not refrigerate the jar, as the olive oil will solidify.

Olives

Elies
Ελιές

Place olives into a bowl. Add the orange rind, lemon rind, bay leaves, salt, red chili flakes, and rosemary. Mix the ingredients well and place them into a jar. Pour in enough vinegar to fill the jar ¾ of the way. Top with olive oil. Close the lid and allow the olives to marinate for a minimum of 4 hours. The olives can be stored at room temperature for up to 1 month.

GLUTEN-FREE
MAKES: 1 JAR
«500 G / 17 OZ.»

250 g (8.8 oz./0.5 lb.) Kalamata olives

250 g (8.8 oz./0.5 lb.) green olives

1 strip of orange rind, 5 cm (2 in.)

1 strip of lemon rind, 5 cm (2 in.)

2 bay leaves

Pinch of salt

Pinch of red chili flakes

1 sprig fresh rosemary, 5 cm (2 in.)

Olive oil

Red wine or apple cider vinegar

Certainly one of the most fundamental foods, bread cannot be absent from a Greek table. If you have bread, extra virgin olive oil, and some cheese, you are set for a great meal. Greeks eat bread at every meal, and we even turn our day-old bread into rusks (stale bread that is baked to make it even harder), which we dip into milk or top with cheese or honey. I enjoy making many different breads, but this one is a simple version that even inexperienced bakers can master. My mother always made bread for us, and she insisted on using whole wheat flour. As much as I love "brown bread," as we called it, I confess that a good white bread with various seeds (to soothe my conscience) also goes down very well. My grandmother only wanted white bread with a good crust. I like Grandma's idea!

Sesame and Fennel Seed Bread

Psomi me Glikaniso kai Sousami

Ψωμί με Γλυκάνισο και Σουσάμι

MAKES: 1 LOAF
TIME: 2 HOURS, 15 MINUTES

- 4 cups all-purpose flour
- 1 tablespoon salt
- ¼ cup sesame seeds
- 3 tablespoons fennel seeds
- 1½ tablespoons instant yeast
- 2–3 cups water, or more if needed

Into a large bowl, add the flour, salt, seeds, and yeast. Slowly add the water, 1 cup at a time, and start to mix the ingredients together with a wooden spoon. (If the dough is too dry, keep adding water. If it is too wet, add more flour.)

Place the dough on a floured surface and knead it until it is soft (5–10 minutes). Transfer the dough to a floured bowl. Cover the bowl, put it in a warm location, and allow the dough to rise for approximately 35 minutes or until it has doubled in size.

Once the dough has risen, knock out the air by punching the dough 3–4 times. Roll it out on a lightly floured surface, shape it into a loaf, and place it into an oiled, 21cm (8 in.) loaf tin or a traditional proving bowl. Cover the dough again and allow it to rise for another 35 minutes.

Preheat the oven to 220°C (428°F).

For crustier bread, put your dough into a preheated Dutch oven (rather than a loaf tin) that has been preheated in the oven for 20 minutes. Bake the bread, covered, for the first 35 minutes, and then uncover it and bake it for another 20 minutes. Alternatively, bake the bread in a loaf tin for 30 minutes or until it is golden brown and sounds hollow when tapped underneath.

Suggestion: To make olive bread, replace the seeds with ¾ cup chopped Kalamata olives.

Riganada is the entrée that relates closest to an Italian bruschetta, though not shy in its portion and its assortment of flavors. It is commonly made with rusks (hard, stale bread). The bread is soaked in a little water and then topped with an array of fresh vegetables and a generous drizzling of extra virgin olive oil. A meal in itself, this is a staple of Kephalonia.

Greek Bruschetta

Riganada
Ριγανάδα

MAKES: 3 SERVINGS
TIME: 15 MINUTES

2 barley rusks*

½ red onion, finely chopped

1 green bell pepper, diced

½ cup Kalamata olives, sliced

2 medium ripe tomatoes, finely chopped

170 g (5.9 oz./0.37 lb.) crumbled feta cheese

¼ cup finely chopped flat-leaf parsley

1 tablespoon dried oregano

¼ cup olive oil

2 tablespoons red wine vinegar

Salt, to taste

Hold the rusks under the kitchen tap, allowing the water to run directly on 1 side (as the water will seep through to the bottom) for 10 seconds; set them aside.

Combine all the other ingredients in a bowl and mix them well. Taste and adjust the seasoning. The mixture must not be dry. If it is, add a little more olive oil.

Top the rusks generously with the mixture and serve immediately.

—

*Barley rusks are available from most international delicatessens.

When I need to relax, I head to my kitchen and open the enormous jar of flour that sits on my counter. I know that as soon as I start to make dough, I will have plenty of energy. Sounds crazy, I know, but it's true. I love making pastry.

This particular dough is an absolute winner. It comes together very easily and does not need a lot of fussing over. Its texture is lovely, thanks to the Greek yogurt and olive oil. The coldness of the yogurt is very enjoyable to work with. I have made thousands of these pies over many years and have yet to be tired of eating them. I often double the quantity and freeze them. These little pies make great gifts or appetizers.

Yogurt Pastry Miniature Cheese Pies

Tiropitakia me Zimi Yiaourtiou
Τυροπιτάκια με Ζύμη Γιαουρτιού

MAKES: 65 PIECES
TIME: 1 HOUR, 30 MINUTES

DOUGH

1 cup olive oil

1 cup Greek yogurt

1 cup whole milk

½ tablespoon salt

1 egg

4–5 cups all-purpose flour

FILLING

250 g (8 oz./0.55 lb.) crumbled feta cheese

90 g (3 oz./0.2 lb.) ricotta cheese

1 teaspoon dried mint

3 tablespoons olive oil

EGG WASH

1 egg yolk

2 tablespoons whole milk

¼ cup black or white sesame seeds to garnish

Preheat the oven to 190°C (374°F).

Place the oil, yogurt, milk, salt, and egg into a bowl. Whisk the ingredients to combine. Slowly add the flour (a little at a time as it may not all be needed), stirring with a wooden spoon until dough has formed. Place the dough on a floured surface and knead it until the dough no longer sticks to your hands. Add additional flour as required. It will come together very easily. Allow the dough to rest for 15 minutes.

In a separate bowl, combine the filling ingredients. Mix well and set aside.

After the dough has rested, roll it out to no more than ½ cm (0.2 in.) thick. Cut out rounds with a 6 cm (2.3 in.) cookie cutter.

Add 1 teaspoon of the filling mixture to each round. Fold each round in half, sealing the edges with a fork. Place the pies on a baking tray.

Combine the egg yolk with the milk and, using a pastry brush, brush each round with the egg wash. Sprinkle sesame seeds over each round.

Bake the cheese pies for 15–20 minutes or until they are golden.

When I think of Greek sausages, my mother's brother's recipe comes to mind. Uncle Jim is a master in the kitchen, and he is the go-to man for the most authentic meals from the Peloponnese. As I have previously mentioned, the Peloponnese consume a lot of pork, and this recipe is a very common one. Pork, fennel, and orange sausages are moist and flavorful.

Sausage making is not that difficult. Think of a sausage as a classy meatball. In fact, that's all it is, with the exception of the casings and different flavors. These sausages are well worth the effort. Double the batch and freeze it. The thing to remember for this recipe is the ratio: 60 percent pork belly and 40 percent pork butt.

Pork, Fennel, and Orange Sausages

Hirina Loukanika me Glikaniso kai Portokali
Χοιρινά Λουκάνικα με Γλυκάνισο και Πορτοκάλι

GLUTEN-FREE
MAKES: 20 PIECES
PREPARATION TIME: 40 MINUTES; ALLOW TO SIT 2 HOURS OR OVERNIGHT
TIME: 10 MINUTES ON A GRILL

680 g (24 oz./1.5 lb.) pork butt, ground

1½ kg (53 oz./3.3 lb.) pork belly, ground

3 orange rinds, diced

3 tablespoons fennel seeds, crushed with a mortar and pestle

10 garlic cloves, minced

1 tablespoon black pepper

2 tablespoons mild paprika

4 tablespoons salt

2 cups white wine

Casings* (keep refrigerated until needed)

For the best results, ensure that all the ingredients are cold and that you work quickly.

Ask your butcher to coarsely grind the meat if you do not have your own grinder. A chunkier consistency is best for these sausages.

In a large bowl, combine the meats with all the remaining ingredients except the casings. Mix the ingredients by hand or with a stand mixer fitted with the paddle attachment until the mixture is sticky and starts to bind together. To test the seasoning, take a small amount of the mixture and roll it into a meatball. Pan fry the meatball in a little olive oil. Taste the meatball and adjust the seasoning if needed. Place the mixture in the refrigerator for 30 minutes.

Remove the casings from the refrigerator and attach to a funnel, or if using a stand mixer, attach the appropriate nozzle. Stuff all the casings before making the links. Gently twist the casings where you want the links to end, gently securing the twists with a piece of kitchen string.

Allow the sausages to dry for a minimum of 2 hours or, better yet, overnight. If the room is warm, dry them for only 1 hour and then refrigerate them on a tray. You want to draw out as much moisture as possible. Place the sausages into a container and use them within a week (or freeze them immediately for use as desired). These sausages are best grilled and served with pita bread and tzatziki.

Tip: Without the casings, this mixture can be used for meatballs. Roll the meat into balls and lightly pan fry or grill them.

*Casings may be purchased from a butcher.

My grandmother always made an amazing cinnamon-stewed cauliflower that is embedded in my brain. Nonetheless, I decided to undertake my mother's cauliflower. She combined feta and cauliflower and steamed them together. Liking the idea, I decided to bake the cauliflower to attain a charred effect, which once again highlights the versatility of feta cheese alongside the mellowness of the cauliflower. This recipe works extremely well as a side dish or a meze.

Cauliflower with Feta Cheese

Kounoupidi me Feta
Κουνουπίδι με Φέτα

GLUTEN-FREE
MAKES: 4-5 SERVINGS
TIME: 55 MINUTES

1 cauliflower, cut into florets

¾ cup olive oil

Salt, to taste

Black pepper, to taste

½ cup bread crumbs (preferably panko crumbs; omit for a gluten-free version)

½ cup kefalograviera cheese*

¾ cup crumbled feta cheese

1 teaspoon dried oregano

Preheat the oven to 210°C (410°F).

Place the cauliflower florets into a shallow baking tray. Top with the olive oil, salt, and pepper. Bake the florets for approximately 30 minutes. The cauliflower should be slightly caramelized and partially cooked. Remove it from the oven and sprinkle it with the bread crumbs, kefalograviera cheese, feta cheese, and oregano. Return the cauliflower to the oven and continue to bake it until it is golden and the cheeses have melted. Serve this dish as a side.

—

Kefalograviera cheese is available at most international delicatessens. Parmesan cheese may be used as a substitute.

TWO

The Saucepan and the Pan

Tis Katsarolas kai tou Tiganiou
Της Κατσαρόλας και του Τηγανιού

Roasted Capsicum (Bell Pepper) Salad

Peloponnese Red Eggs (GF)

Olive Oil Fried Potatoes with Egg and Feta (GF)

Dolmadakia (GF)

Capsicum and Apple Salsa (GF)

Chickpea Soup (GF option)

Meatball and Rice Soup (GF)

Cinnamon Chicken with Lemon Potatoes (GF)

Long Green Beans with Olive Oil (GF)

Chicken and Rice Soup (GF)

Fried Whitebait (GF)

Lentil Soup (GF)

Kephalonian Beef Stew

Bean Soup (GF)

Rabbit and Onion Stew (GF)

Eggplant, Sausage, and Cream Rolls (GF)

Flatbreads

Cabbage Rolls with Lemon (GF)

Lemon-Dressed Potato Salad

GF denotes gluten-free recipes

The Saucepan and the Pan

What is a kitchen without its pots and pans? Cast iron and stainless steel varieties fill my mother's kitchen. She is a master at using stainless-steel pans. She has her technique of cooking with them perfectly down pat, making sure there are no nonstick varieties in her home. The majority of her collection is large pots, big enough to cook for an army. I don't recall her ever cooking for two or three people—she cooks for a crowd!

Not surprisingly, the first gift I received when I got engaged was a very expensive set of pots with a lifetime warranty. Maybe that was a hint, but whatever the case, I love them. I have added numerous others to my collection since then, and I delight in cooking meals on the stove (a very important part of Greek cooking). A pan and saucepan are vital. We fry fish and make sauces, soups, stews, and puddings on the stove. A major component of stove-top cooking comes from a selection of foods called *ladera*, meaning "oily." This is a term used for meals that are peasant-style and that are commonly cooked on the stove, usually in a tomato sauce with plenty of olive oil, hence the word oily. When cooked correctly, *ladera* dishes are so appetizing. They highlight the versatility and the beauty of olive oil. The crucial thing is to cook the food sufficiently so that the juices evaporate and what is left is a shiny layer of olive oil. Olive oil is not used sparingly in these dishes. So, with a pot, a pan, and a stove, get ready to cook Greek-style with these recipes.

I shouldn't call this just a salad; rather, it's a condiment for any time. Not only are these sweet red capsicums a great side dish or antipasto accompaniment but they are also deliciously addictive on top of toast drizzled with olive oil, a sprinkling of oregano, and crumbled feta cheese. As simple as this recipe sounds, it is refreshingly wonderful.

Roasted Capsicum (Bell Pepper) Salad

Piperies Psites sto Fourno
Πιπεριές Ψητές στο Φούρνο

GLUTEN-FREE
MAKES: 3 SERVINGS
TIME: 35 MINUTES TO ROAST/
10 MINUTES TO ASSEMBLE

4 large red capsicums (bell peppers)

½ cup olive oil

2 garlic cloves, minced

½ cup chopped flat leaf parsley

¼ cup crumbled feta cheese

Dash of balsamic vinegar (optional)

4–5 small mint leaves (optional)

Preheat the oven to 190°C (374°F).

Place the capsicums on a baking tray. Bake them for 30–40 minutes or until they are blistered and soft. If they are blackened, do not be alarmed—that is okay. Remove the tray from the oven and place the peppers in a bowl. Cover the bowl with cling wrap and set it aside for 5–10 minutes (the heat will create steam, allowing the peppers' skins to come off more easily).

Peel away the skins and seeds. Cut the peppers into long, thick strips and place them in a bowl. If there are some charred pieces, keep them, as they give a lovely flavor to the dish.

In a small saucepan, heat the olive oil and add the garlic. Cook the garlic for 2 minutes or until it is fragrant. Pour the oil and garlic over the capsicums, add the parsley, and mix gently to combine all the ingredients.

Place the salad on a flat platter and top with the feta cheese and the optional balsamic vinegar and mint leaves.

To store the salad, place it in a glass jar or container and refrigerate it for up to 1 week.

This is beyond question one of my childhood picks for that quick, healthy snack. We rarely ate fast food, so Mum would do her best to make vegetables taste amazing—and it worked! My sister and I would grate fresh summer tomatoes, and Mum would then finish the dish. It's oozy from the eggs, it's juicy from the tomatoes, it's tasty from the caramelized onions, it's quick, and it's super healthy! Get yourself a loaf of bread (or a gluten-free alternative) and get ready to dip into this dish of comfort. I remember that as children we would fight over the last portion so that we could wipe the serving dish clean with our bread. Traditionally, there is no onion added (but I choose to differ), and in regions like Kephalonia, the eggs are always scrambled, not left whole. This is great for a meze, breakfast, lunch, or even a light snack when tomatoes are in season. Serve this recipe hot or at room temperature.

Peloponnese Red Eggs

Strapatsada Pelopponisou
Στραπατσάδα Πελοποννήσου

GLUTEN-FREE
MAKES: 2 SERVINGS
TIME: 20 MINUTES

¼ cup olive oil

½ onion, diced

¼ teaspoon mild paprika

3 large, very ripe tomatoes, grated

2 eggs

1 teaspoon dried oregano

Salt, to taste

Black pepper, to taste

In a medium pan, heat the olive oil and sauté the onion until it is soft and caramelized. Add the paprika, salt, and grated tomatoes. Allow the mixture to simmer, uncovered, for 10 minutes. When the liquid has evaporated by half, crack 1 egg at a time, dropping it into the pan. Allow the whites to cook (do not overcook them, as you want a runny yolk). Sprinkle the oregano and some cracked pepper on the yolks. Take the pan off the heat, and drizzle a little olive oil over the dish just before serving. This is best served with the pan in the middle of your table so that everyone can serve themselves. Be sure to serve it with crusty bread and feta cheese on the side.

—

For scrambled eggs, beat the 2 eggs in a small bowl and pour them into the pan. With a wooden spoon, mix the eggs throughout the tomato mixture. Cook the eggs until they are well done.

Peloponnese Red Eggs (page 91) & Roasted Capsicum Salad (page 90)

Yes, potatoes fried in olive oil. There are plenty of myths suggesting that olive oil is not good for frying. Truth be told, olive oil is ideal for frying, and it's better for you. There are many oils and fats that, once heated, release unhealthy toxins. The difference and the benefit of frying with olive oil is that it undergoes no significant structural alteration when heated, and it also retains its nutritional value. Its high smoking point (210ºC/410ºF) is significantly greater than the perfect temperature for frying food (180ºC/356ºF).

The smell, the taste, the crunch of perfect fried potatoes definitely cannot be resisted. Remember to heat the oil adequately so that the potatoes retain their crunchy exterior.

Olive Oil Fried Potatoes with Egg and Feta Cheese

Tiganites Patates me Avga kai Tiri Feta
Τηγανιτές Πατάτες με Αυγά και Τυρί Φέτα

GLUTEN-FREE
MAKES: 2 SERVINGS
TIME: 45 MINUTES

Light olive oil for frying (enough to fill your pan ¼ of the way)

2 large potatoes, peeled and cut into fries about 1 cm (0.4 in.) wide

Salt, to taste

2 eggs, whisked

1 teaspoon dried oregano

¼ cup crumbled feta cheese

Cut the potatoes and season them with salt. Heat the oil in a wide pan. Place 1 potato in the oil; if it sizzles, the oil is ready for frying.

Gently add potatoes to the hot oil and fry them, turning once or twice throughout the cooking process so that they brown up evenly. Drain the potatoes and place them on a plate.

Pour the oil out of the frying pan, leaving only 2 tablespoons in it, and then put the potatoes back into the frying pan. Over high heat, drizzle the whisked eggs over the potatoes, tossing once or twice to coat them all. Continue cooking for 1 minute or until the eggs are cooked through. Immediately sprinkle oregano and feta cheese over the potatoes and eggs. Remove from the heat and toss gently. Serve hot.

I love these delicately wrapped vine-leaf packages. Dolmadakia gialantzi (the meat-free variety) are filled with an array of spices, herbs, and rice. One bite, and you get a salty, sour little pop in your mouth amid the spices and rice. This for me is the absolute epitome of the best rolled-up little rice bite. One of the best meze plates you can eat!

There are different varieties of dolmadakia in Greece, some made with meat, sultanas, and pine nuts, but this recipe is the more traditional style adapted from my Uncle Jim. Vine leaves come brined in jars and can be purchased from international delicatessens, or one can use fresh vine leaves that have been blanched in salted water for a few minutes.

Dolmadakia

Dolmadakia
Ντολμαδάκια

GLUTEN-FREE
MAKES: 70 PIECES
TIME: 1 HOUR, 30 MINUTES

Allow the preserved vine leaves to soak in a bowl of cold water for 30 minutes. This will wash off any excess salt. Drain the leaves and layer 1 row in the bottom of a saucepan. This will protect the dolmadakia from sticking to the bottom of the saucepan.

Place the rice, spring onions, onion, mint, parsley, dill, ¾ cup of the olive oil, salt, and pepper in a bowl. Taste a little of the rice to see if there is enough seasoning, adjusting it if needed.

Lay each leaf stem side up and place 1 teaspoon of the rice mixture in its center. Fold the leaf by bringing the sides together, and then roll the leaf to enclose the rice in the leaf. Place each dolmadaki seam side down in the pan. Repeat this process with all the vine leaves, placing them close together in the pan.

Pour the remaining ¾ cup olive oil, boiled water, and lemon juice in the pot. Place a plate that is smaller than the diameter of the pot on top of the dolmadakia so that they don't puff up and open while cooking.

Place a lid on the pot and simmer the dolmadakia over low heat for about 35 minutes or until the water is absorbed and the rice is cooked through. If you are finding that the water is absorbing too quickly, just keep adding a little more boiling water until the dolmadakia are cooked.

Take the pan off the heat and place a clean tea towel on top of it. Place the lid on the towel, and allow the steam to be completely absorbed by the towel.

Dolmadakia can be kept refrigerated for up to 3 days. Serve them with Greek yogurt and an additional squeeze of lemon.

500 g (17.6 oz./1.1 lb.) vine leaves, preserved in brine

2 cups medium-grain rice

2 cups finely chopped spring onion

1 large onion, diced

½ cup finely chopped mint

½ cup finely chopped flat leaf parsley

½ cup finely chopped dill

1½ cups olive oil, divided

1 teaspoon salt

1 teaspoon black pepper

2½ cups boiling water

2 lemons, freshly squeezed

When I was a child, my family had a custom that would occur once a year in our back yard. My family, together with my aunties and uncles, crafted homemade tomato sauce, enough to keep us in supply for a year at a time. My memories of those days are filled with large barrels, endless boxes of plump, red tomatoes, various seasonings, large empty beer bottles, bottle caps, and much noise from all the Greek chatter. Amid the laughter and enjoyment of being together, everyone would assist in preparing and cooking the sauce. It would be a full day outside until hundreds of bottles had been sterilized and filled with amazing tomato sauce.

This recipe is a tiny reproduction of this tradition, with some adaptations my Auntie Margaret and I would make when attempting a smaller volume and using red capsicums and canned tomatoes. I use this recipe for anything that calls for a tomato sauce. I make a big batch while the red capsicums are in season so that I have fresh sauce any time of the year!

Capsicum and Apple Salsa

Saltsa me Kokkini Piperia kai Mila
Σάλτσα με Κόκκινη Πιπεριά και Μήλα

GLUTEN-FREE
MAKES: 3.5 L «118 FL. OZ.»
TIME: 2 HOURS, 30 MINUTES

- 7 Red Delicious apples, peeled, cored, and quartered
- 9 red capsicums (bell peppers), roasted and peeled
- 9 garlic cloves
- 1 cup olive oil
- 3 teaspoons red chili flakes
- 8 large fresh basil leaves
- 4 tablespoons dark brown sugar
- 1 cinnamon quill
- 400 g (14.1 oz. / 0.88 lb.) crushed tomatoes
- 2 teaspoons cinnamon powder
- 700 ml (23.6 fl oz.) tomato puree
- 2 tablespoons salt
- 1 teaspoon freshly ground black pepper

Preheat the oven to 230°C (446°F).

Place the apples in a pot and add ¼ cup water. Simmer the apples until they are soft. Mash them with a potato masher and set them aside.

Place the red capsicums and the garlic cloves in a baking dish. Roast them for 45 minutes or until the capsicums are soft and blistered. Set the baking dish aside to cool. Remove the skins both from the capsicums and the garlic (they come off very easily). Process the capsicums and the garlic in a food processor.

In a large, heavy pot, heat the olive oil and add the capsicum mixture. Sauté the mixture for about 4 minutes. Add the red chili flakes, mashed apples, basil leaves, sugar, cinnamon quill, cinnamon powder, tomato puree, crushed tomatoes, salt, pepper, and an additional 2 cups of water.

Cook the salsa over low heat for about 1 hour or until the sauce has thickened. It should taste sweet and spicy and have a hint of heat.

To preserve the salsa, use jars with a suction top. They could be reused from other jars. Wash and dry them (there is no need to sterilize them). Pour the hot salsa into the jars, cap them, and immediately turn the bottles upside down. Allow them to cool, and then turn right side up. The suction should have sealed the bottles.

By far the best chickpeas I have eaten have been in Greece—they were large, plump, juicy, and almost meat-like. To be more precise, the best chickpeas I have eaten belonged to an auntie on my husband's side of the family. We made an unexpected visit to my husband's hometown of Elefsina, not having told his relatives we were flying in from Australia. Upon arriving at his auntie's front door, we discovered that she had just made a pot of this soup. She was somewhat apologetic for not having something more formal. She needn't have been, because when she filled our soup bowls, it looked amazing. The smell of lemon and oregano hit my nostrils, and I was very keen to try her version of these little white balls. I took my first spoonful and then rather quickly polished off the whole bowl. I couldn't resist and modestly took a second bowlful. It was delightful, and I was surprised at how I had underestimated a pot of chickpea soup. Undoubtedly, lemons picked from a local tree in the Mediterranean did help.

There are two traditional ways to make this soup. One is "white," which is the recipe below. The other version is "red," made with the addition of tomato. Both are delicious. This soup has few ingredients but is pungent in flavor, and it is a complete meal in itself. It is dairy free and bursting with nutritional value.

Chickpea Soup

Revithia
Ρεβίθια

GLUTEN-FREE*
MAKES: 4 SERVINGS
TIME: 50 MINUTES

1 cup dried chickpeas, soaked overnight in cold water with 1 tablespoon baking soda

½ onion, grated

Black pepper, to taste

1 teaspoon dried oregano

3 tablespoons olive oil

1 large lemon, juiced

Salt, to taste

1 slice white crusty bread*

Drain the chickpeas and place them in a pot, covering them with fresh water. Add another 2 cups of water. Add a few grounds of pepper and the grated onion. Allow the chickpeas to boil over medium heat for approximately 45 minutes until they are soft, adding water as necessary to prevent the pot from boiling dry.

Remove half the cooked chickpeas from the pot. With a hand blender, blend the remaining soup to a smooth, creamy consistency. Now return the whole chickpeas to the pot, stirring to combine them with the blended chickpeas. Add salt to taste, oregano, olive oil, and lemon juice. Mix the ingredients well.

Place the bread on top and push it down a little so that it can absorb the soup. Let the bread soak for about 6 minutes.

Serve the soup in bowls, adding a dash of extra olive oil and lemon juice.

—

*Omit the bread for a gluten-free option.

I must confess—I eat this soup all year round. I know soups are generally enjoyed in winter, but I could eat half a pot of this soup in one sitting, regardless of whether it's a cold or hot day. During the summer months, I let the soup cool to room temperature and add a squeeze of cold, fresh lemon juice. During the colder months, I have it steaming hot.

This lemony broth with small, herb-stuffed meatballs floating in the partly clouded rice soup is delicious! The rice helps thicken the soup, creating an emulsion and a fluffy yet tangy foam. My mother would make this soup using fresh parsley from the garden, giving the meatballs a real punch of flavor.

GLUTEN-FREE
MAKES: 6-8 SERVINGS
TIME: 1 HOUR

Meatball and Rice Soup

Giouvarlakia
Γιουβαρλάκια

BROTH

2 L (67.6 fl. oz.) water

2 tablespoons olive oil

1 teaspoon salt

MEATBALLS

500 g (17.6 oz. /1.1 lb.) minced beef

1 large onion, finely chopped

½ cup finely chopped flat leaf parsley

½ cup finely chopped mint

1 egg

1½ teaspoon salt

1 teaspoon pepper

1 cup medium-grain Arborio rice

¼ cup olive oil

SAUCE

2 large lemons, juiced

2 eggs

Place the water, 2 tablespoons of olive oil, and 1 teaspoon salt in a large pot. Bring the water to a boil and then reduce the heat, allowing the water to simmer while you prepare the meatballs.

In a bowl, combine the beef, onion, parsley, mint, egg, salt, pepper, rice, and olive oil. Mix the ingredients well and start rolling approximately 50 small meatballs with your palms (the balls should be a little smaller than a golf ball). Place the meatballs in a single layer on a plate until you have made them all.

Drop all the meatballs gently into the simmering water. Allow them to simmer for 35 minutes or until the meatballs are totally cooked through. Taste a meatball together with some water and adjust seasoning if required.

Separate the eggs and whisk the 2 egg whites in a bowl until they are thick and fluffy but not too stiff. Add the yolks and the lemon juice. Whisk the ingredients again to incorporate them. Take 2 large ladles of water from the pot of meatballs and whisk them into the sauce. Pour the mixture into the soup. Stir the soup to incorporate the sauce and then turn the stove off, putting a lid on the pot. Allow the soup to stand about 10 minutes so that it thickens. Serve the soup with a wedge of lemon on the side and some cracked black pepper.

This is a dish that gets my senses buzzing and brings back the joyful emotions of a special time.

Sitting at our kitchen table alongside my grandmother Angeliki, I shuffle my chair closer to the table, being careful not to trip over her walking stick that is lying between both chairs. She takes a deep breath and says to my mum, "Toula, it's ready. Let's eat!"

Amazingly, she is spot-on. She learned to cook by sense and smell. The eyeballing technique and the use of the senses is such an art form in cooking. I also inhale deeply through my nostrils as I create a particular sense in my brain, trying to work out the trick my grandmother uses. The aroma is delightful but also puzzling. I try to determine what the distinct smell is. There is a sharp lemon smell but also the aroma of cinnamon.

The pot is brought before us, and we dig into this tasteful peasant dish. Grandmother is speechless but murmuring sounds of satisfaction. I imagine that her thoughts are taking her back to her village in Greece, where her large family, living through wars and famine, cooked this recipe over coals. This dish, carrying emotions from one generation to the next, is best served warm.

Cinnamon Chicken with Lemon Potatoes

Kotopoulo Giahni
Κοτόπουλο Γιαχνί

GLUTEN-FREE
MAKES: 4–6 SERVINGS
TIME: 1 HOUR, 30 MINUTES

½ cup olive oil

1 onion, diced

1 kg (35.2 oz. /2.2 lb.) small chicken drumsticks

1 tablespoon salt

1 teaspoon black pepper

1 tablespoon dried oregano

2 large lemons, juiced

4 large potatoes, each cut into 8 pieces

1½ teaspoons cinnamon powder

Light olive oil for frying

In a wide sauté pan that has a lid, sauté the onion in the olive oil until it is soft and translucent. Add the chicken and cook until it is well browned. Add the salt, pepper, oregano, and lemon juice. Pour boiled water into the pan to cover the chicken. Taste the water mixture. It must be well salted and have a strong lemon bite. If it doesn't, add another lemon and more salt. Cook the chicken over low heat, uncovered, until the juice is reduced to a little more than half.

While the chicken cooks, fill another pan to the halfway point with light olive oil (never fill a pan more than halfway). Heat the oil and fry the potatoes. To ensure the oil is hot enough, place 1 potato into the oil, and when it sizzles, the oil is ready. Do not cook the potatoes right through; 3 to 4 minutes before they are fully cooked, drain them and place them straight into the chicken mixture. Let them cook together with the chicken for about 3 minutes. Turn off the heat, sprinkle the cinnamon powder on top, and put a lid on the pan. Allow the potatoes to soak up all the juices for about 10 minutes, and then serve the dish.

When I think of long green beans, I automatically recall the hundreds of times as a young girl I would sit at the kitchen table with a bowl in front of me and a small knife and a peeler in my hand. Ever so slowly I would snip the ends off the beans, while mum looked over my shoulders making sure I was cutting them correctly. I would often complain about the fiddly task and question why we did not just buy frozen beans. Mum in her persuasive manner never budged but rather lovingly explained the benefit of buying fresh groceries over packaged and the benefit of being patient to take the time to prepare food. It was not a chore but a joy! So the key to this tasty dish is to buy beans when in season and not hold back on the olive oil. Traditionally, the star of these oil-based dishes is the olive oil. It seems quite excessive, but olive oil is a good fat, and with the combination of olive oil and the vegetable juices, this recipe transforms into a tasty vegetable dish. The addition of baby peas and fresh tomatoes makes it sweet and appetizing. I grew up with this version, and I wouldn't think of changing the memory from my mind.

Long Green Bean Stew with Olive Oil

Fasolakia Ladera
Φασολάκια Λαδερά

GLUTEN-FREE
MAKES: 6 SERVINGS
TIME: 1 HOUR, 30 MINUTES

¾ cup olive oil

1 large onion, sliced

2 large garlic cloves, minced

2 tablespoons tomato paste

500 g (17.6 oz. /1.1 lb.) long green beans, ends trimmed

1 large potato, peeled and quartered

¾ cup butternut pumpkin, cut into big chunks

1 large red capsicum (bell pepper), cut into thin strips

345 g (12 oz. /0.76 lb.) sweet baby peas

1 teaspoon cinnamon powder

1 teaspoon mild paprika

5 large ripe tomatoes, grated

Salt, to taste

Black pepper, to taste

Start by cutting the ends off the beans. If using the stringy, flat beans, remove the strings by running a potato peeler down the sides. Cut the beans in half or in thirds.

In a wide casserole dish, heat the olive oil over medium heat. Add onions and garlic, sautéing them until they are soft and fragrant. Add the tomato paste and cook for 1 minute, mixing it into the onion mixture. Add the beans and cook for another 4 minutes, stirring so they don't stick to the bottom of the pan. Add the potato, pumpkin, capsicum, peas, cinnamon, paprika, and grated tomatoes. Season this mixture well and cover it with water.

Cook the stew, covered, over low to medium heat for 30–45 minutes (if it seems to be drying out, add another cup of water). At the end of this time, uncover the pan and cook the stew for another 30 minutes or until the water has evaporated by half, the beans are tender, and the oil has come to the surface. Serve this stew with feta cheese.

Every time I tell my husband I'm making this soup, he starts to make kissing sounds with his lips. This relates to the egg and lemon sauce that is added to the soup. Greeks hold that if you make these sounds while whisking the eggs, they won't curdle when poured into the hot soup. Regardless of whether this is a fact or just a myth, I love the tradition of hearing it. This soup is very smooth and fluffy to the palate, and it is enriched by this tangy lemon sauce. This is a Greek's version of chicken soup!

Chicken & Rice Soup

Kotosoupa Avgolemono
Κοτόσουπα Αυγολέμονο

GLUTEN-FREE
MAKES: 6 SERVINGS
TIME: 2 HOURS, 50 MINUTES

2½ – 3 L (84–100 fl. oz.) water, enough to just cover the chicken

1 medium organic chicken, skin on

1 celery stalk, whole

1 large carrot, whole

1 onion, whole

5 peppercorns

2 tablespoons salt

2 bay leaves

1 cup medium-grain Arborio rice

2 large lemons

2 eggs

Place the water, chicken, celery, carrot, onion, peppercorns, salt, and bay leaves into a large pot. Allow the water to come to a boil and then lower the heat, simmering it for approximately 2 hours. Skim off any foam or scum that rises to the top. The chicken should be fully cooked and falling off the bone. Remove the chicken from the pot and shred the meat. Set it aside.

Strain the stock through a sieve into a clean pot. Discard the vegetables. Bring the stock back to a light boil. Add the rice and cook over medium heat until the rice is fully cooked, approximately 15–20 minutes.

Take the eggs and separate the whites from the yolks. Whisk the 2 egg whites until they are thick and frothy but not too stiff. Add the yolks and the lemon juice, whisking them together to mix well. Take 2 large ladles of the stock and whisk these into the sauce vigorously so that the eggs won't curdle. Pour the mixture into the soup. Stir the soup to combine the ingredients and then turn the stove off immediately, putting a lid on the pot. Allow the soup to sit for about 10 minutes so that it thickens. Serve this soup with a good grind of cracked pepper, a splash of lemon juice, and some shredded chicken.

You cannot sit in a Greek tavern without having a serving of fried whitebait. The crispiness from the batter, along with the tang from a squeeze of lemon juice, makes this dish a starter you cannot resist on a summer's day or night. With only a few ingredients, this simple yet healthy snack is delicious, and it will bring you one step closer to that Greek atmosphere. Always buy fish that is fresh and does not smell fishy. Fresh fish always smells like the sea. If you can't find whitebait, anchovies or sardines are a great substitute and are cooked exactly the same way.

Fried Whitebait

Lithrini sto Tigani
Λιθρίνι στο Τηγάνι

MAKES: 2 SERVINGS
TIME: 20 MINUTES

250 g (8.8 oz. /0.55 lb.) whitebait, gutted and cleaned*

Salt, to taste

¾ cup all-purpose flour

2 cups light olive oil, for frying

1 lemon, juiced

1 tablespoon dried oregano

Place the cleaned whitebait on a tray and dry them with a paper towel so that most of the moisture gets absorbed—this ensures that the fish does not splatter when placed in the hot oil.

Take a plastic food bag (or use a deep bowl) and combine the fish, salt, and flour. Close the bag and shake it to ensure the flour covers all the fish well. If using a bowl, use your fingers to gently toss the fish in the flour.

Heat the olive oil in a shallow pan. To test whether the oil is hot enough to fry, take 1 fish and lower it into the pan. If it starts to sizzle, the oil is ready. Gently shake off any excess flour from the fish, drop them into the pan, and fry them until golden. Remove the fish with a slotted spoon and drain them on some paper towels. To serve the whitebait, add a wedge of lemon, a pinch of Greek oregano, and a grinding of extra salt. Serve them immediately.

—

*Your fishmonger should be able to gut and clean the fish.

Every Greek household makes a version of lentil soup. This dish is pronounced "fah-kess." It is high in protein, gluten-free, and totally vegan. This started as my mum's recipe, until I experimented a little and found a take on it that I enjoy a little more (sorry, Mum). Be sure to use dried Greek oregano in this soup. It is more aromatic and intense in flavor. To serve the soup, add a splash of red wine vinegar, a couple of olives, and a drizzle of olive oil. These additions definitely complete the soup. Lentils marry well with many flavor options such as pumpkin and rosemary. In this case, I have added orzo pasta.

Lentil Soup

Fakes
Φακές

GLUTEN-FREE*
MAKES: 4 SERVINGS
TIME: 1 HOUR

1 cup brown lentils

2 bay leaves

6 cups water

1 medium onion, diced

½ cup olive oil

2 tablespoons tomato paste

1 teaspoon mild paprika

Salt, to taste

Black pepper, to taste

1 tablespoon dried Greek oregano

¼ cup orzo pasta*

Red wine vinegar, for serving

Kalamata olives, for serving

Place the lentils, bay leaves, and water into a pot. Cook over medium heat until the lentils are soft and cooked.

In another pot, sauté the onion with olive oil until it is translucent. Add tomato paste and cook the mixture for 2 minutes, stirring to loosen the paste. Add the paprika, salt, and pepper and cook for another 5 minutes.

Pour the cooked lentils and all the water into the tomato mixture and mix well. If the consistency is too thick, add 1–2 cups of boiled water. To this, add the oregano and orzo pasta and cook for another 10–15 minutes or until the orzo is cooked.

Check the seasoning and adjust it if needed. Serve with a drizzle of olive oil, a splash of vinegar, and a few olives in each bowl.

—

*Orzo pasta is rice-size pasta, also known by the name risoni. Orzo can be purchased anywhere pasta is sold. Omit it for a gluten-free meal.

Pastitsada is a traditional meal served in Kephalonia and the surrounding islands. It is a traditional Sunday dish. There are a few variations, but all in all, the stew is made of a variety of spices, and it is served with thick, tubular spaghetti whose tube-like shape allows the sauce to seep into the holes. They say that the stew requires no fewer than nine spices in total. My mother, being from the Peloponnese, substitutes a rooster for the beef. The cooking directions are exactly the same except that it has a quicker cooking time. To serve this dish, add a liberal sprinkling of *mizithra* cheese. The stew is best when eaten warm.

Kephalonian Beef Stew

Kefalonitiki Pastitsada
Κεφαλλονίτικη Παστιτσάδα

In a large, heavy pot (or a large clay pot), heat the olive oil with the onions and garlic, sautéing them until they are soft. Add the meat and brown it well. (Do not skip this step—the flavor is in the browning of the meat.) Add all the remaining ingredients and cook the stew over low to medium heat for 2–3 hours or until the meat is tender and the juices have thickened slightly. Taste it and adjust the seasoning if needed.

In a pot of salted water, boil the pasta as directed on the package. Drain the spaghetti and put it back into the pot. In a small frying pan, heat the olive oil until it starts to become fragrant and smoke slightly. Carefully pour the oil into the pasta, tossing it to coat it well.

Serve the pasta topped with the beef stew, sprinkling it liberally with mizithra cheese.

—

Mizithra cheese (purchased from international delicatessens) is a hard cheese made from unpasteurized fresh goat's milk. Parmesan cheese may be used as a substitute.

Make-ahead tip: The stew can be made a day ahead. Refrigerate it and then slowly reheat it as required. The stew also freezes well.

MAKES: 4 SERVINGS
TIME: 2-3 HOURS, 15 MINUTES

½ cup olive oil

1 large onion, diced

3 large garlic cloves, minced

500 g (17.6 oz. /1.1 lb.) beef, cut into bite-size pieces

1 strip orange rind (be careful not to add the white pith, as this will give it a bitter aftertaste)

2 teaspoons castor (superfine) sugar

¼ teaspoon ground cloves

1 teaspoon ground mild paprika

1 teaspoon ground nutmeg

1 teaspoon ground cumin

1 teaspoon ground black pepper

1 teaspoon ground cinnamon

2 dried bay leaves

1 cinnamon quill

5 whole cloves

4 allspice berries

Salt, to taste

2 cups tomato puree

2 cups water

500 g (16 oz. /1.1 lb.) tubular spaghetti

¼ cup olive oil

Mizithra* cheese

What Greek child can forget the good old bowl of bean soup cooking away in the kitchen? As a child I never appreciated this soup, but I have grown to love it, and I enjoy its nutritional value and taste. It is gluten- and dairy-free and a much-loved vegan alternative to a meat soup. This soup is so traditional that I could not think of writing a Greek cookbook without it. I have added butternut pumpkin and fresh basil for that extra punch of flavor. This is a one-pot wonder—get it on the stove and forget about it.

GLUTEN-FREE
MAKES: 6–8 SERVINGS
TIME: 2 HOURS, 30 MINUTES

2 cups medium-sized cannellini beans

½ cup olive oil

1 large onion, diced

1 cup chopped celery

1 large carrot, thinly sliced

2 teaspoons mild paprika

3 teaspoons dried oregano

1 tablespoon tomato paste

½ cup tomato puree

2 medium potatoes, finely cubed

1 cup chopped butternut pumpkin

1.25 L (42.2 fl. oz.) water

2 bay leaves

3 fresh basil leaves

1 teaspoon black pepper

1 tablespoon salt, or to taste

Bean Soup

Fasolada
Φασολάδα

Soak the beans overnight in water and drain them in the morning.

In a large pot, sauté the onions, celery, and carrots in the olive oil until the vegetables are soft.

Add the paprika, oregano, and tomato paste and cook the mixture for about 5 minutes.

Add the beans, tomato puree, potatoes, pumpkin, bay leaves, basil leaves, pepper, and enough water to cover the ingredients. Do not add salt until the soup is cooked, otherwise the salt will harden the beans and they will take longer to cook. Cook the soup, covered, over low to medium heat for 60–80 minutes or until the beans, potatoes, and pumpkin are soft and tender.

With the back of a spoon, mash the pumpkin against the sides of the pot so that it thickens the soup. Add salt to taste and serve the soup with thick, crusty bread (omit it for a gluten-free option), a bowl of olives, and feta cheese on the side.

—

Suggestion: If you like spice, add a pinch of dried red chili flakes.

If you were to ask Greeks how they would cook rabbit, no doubt they would immediately say, "Stifado." It is a stew cooked in wine and enhanced with cinnamon, clove, orange, and sweet pickling onions. The low heat and slow cooking time ensure that the rabbit is cooked to perfection, the meat falling off the bone. This is definitely my favorite meal to eat. I love the smell of it cooking, I love rabbit meat, I love the sweet pickled onions, I love the juices of the dish—I just love it all!

My father was a hunter, so we often got fresh rabbits from our twenty-acre farm. I was eight years old when I asked if my dad would teach me to shoot. I wanted to hunt my own rabbits. Dad was excited that his little girl wanted to learn to shoot; he nestled the double-barrel gun into my shoulder and directed me to aim. What I remember next was a sudden pain and a lovely blue bruise.

If you have never eaten rabbit, don't be intimidated by it. It is a delicious meat, though you could substitute veal or beef in this recipe. Ensure you cover your casserole with a lid.

Rabbit and Onion Stew

Lago Stifado

Λαγός Στιφάδο

GLUTEN-FREE
MAKES: 5 SERVINGS
TIME: 3 HOURS, 30 MINUTES

2 kg (70.5 oz. /4.4 lb.) pickling onions, peeled*

1 cup olive oil

1 whole rabbit, cut into 6 pieces

2 cinnamon quills

8 garlic cloves, peeled

4 bay leaves

10 peppercorns

Salt, to taste

½ cup red wine vinegar

¾ cup red wine

3 tablespoons tomato paste, diluted in ¼ cup water

1 strip orange rind, 5 cm (2 in.)

In a large pot (I cook this in a Dutch oven), heat the olive oil. Season the rabbit with salt. Add the meat to the oil and brown it well. Add the onions on top of the meat, but do not mix them together; the meat should be on the bottom. Add the remaining ingredients along with 1 cup of water (the onions will also release their own juices while cooking). Cover the pot and allow the ingredients to simmer over low heat for about 2½ – 3 hours. The onions should be soft, caramelized, and reduced by half.

Serve the stew with some crusty bread or some fried potatoes.

—

Pearl onions, which are small, mild, white onions, can be substituted for pickling onions.

Tip: To speed up the onion-peeling process, blanch the onions in boiling water for 5 minutes. This will help the skins peel away easily.

The appearance of this entrée seems to always remind me immediately of something from the '60s: my mother's choice of a bold-colored plate, a black-and-white photograph of my slender father as a young adult, and the thought of his choosing to eat this comfort food only in small amounts. It's so deliciously decadent that as he would say, "You only need a small piece, Ruth; moderation is the key." So this dish, with its few ingredients, is tastefully divine. The mixture of cream, sausage, and cheese is just the perfect side to any dish. If you prefer, you can omit the cream and add 2 cups of crushed tomatoes. Always fry eggplants in olive oil and liberally sprinkle them with salt.

Eggplant, Sausage, and Cream Rolls

Melitzanes Rolo
Μελιτζάνες Ρολό

GLUTEN-FREE
MAKES: 16 ENTRÉE-SIZE ROLLS
TIME: 1 HOUR, 15 MINUTES

Preheat the oven to 220°C (428°F).

Fry the eggplants in a little olive oil until they are golden on both sides. Season them with some salt and set them aside. Fry the sausages until they are golden.

To assemble the rolls, place an eggplant slice on a work surface. Sprinkle 1 tablespoon of cheese on it and place a piece of sausage close to the end of the eggplant strip. Roll the strip up tightly to enclose the ingredients and place the roll in a baking dish that is 23 cm by 17 cm (9 in. by 6.6 in.), seam side down.

Repeat this process with the remaining eggplant strips, placing them side by side in the dish. Pour the cream over the rolls and sprinkle them with the remainder of the grated cheese.

Bake at 220°C (428°F) for 30–40 minutes until the rolls are golden and bubbly. Serve warm.

—

Kefalograviera cheese can be substituted with mozzarella cheese.

2 large eggplants, sliced lengthwise into ½ cm (0.2 in.) strips

Salt, to taste

Olive oil for shallow frying

2 chorizo or Greek sausages, sliced into 1 cm (0.4 in.) pieces

350 ml (12 fl oz.) thickened cream (heavy cream)

150 g (5.2 oz./0.33 lb.) grated kefalograviera* cheese

My husband and I love these feta cheese flatbreads. We make them regularly in our home. As they cook in the olive oil, they start to puff up, and the cheese starts to melt. The ingredients are few, and the whole process is quick and easy. Be warned: they are addictive. This is my mother-in-law's recipe from the region of Edessa. They are extremely versatile. Use them for souvlakia or pita for dips, eat them hot straight out of the pan, or if you have a sweet tooth like my husband, top them with a drizzle of honey and a sprinkle of cinnamon. I double the quantity, because surely fourteen are not enough!

Flatbreads

Pontiaka Pisia
Ποντιακά Πισία

MAKES: 14 FLATBREADS
TIME: 55 MINUTES

4 cups all-purpose flour

2 teaspoons instant yeast

5 tablespoons olive oil, divided, plus more for shallow frying

1½ teaspoons salt

2 cups lukewarm water (this is approximate—depending on your flour, you may need a little more or less)

375 g (13.2 oz. /0.82 lb.) feta cheese, crumbled

2 teaspoons dried oregano

Mix together the flour, yeast, 2 tablespoons of the olive oil, and salt. Slowly add the water, mixing the ingredients together with a wooden spoon to make dough. It must not be too sticky or too dry. When the dough has come together, move the dough to a lightly floured board or bench and knead it well for approximately 8 minutes. The dough should be soft and smooth. Cover it and allow it to rest for 20 minutes.

Combine the cheese, the remaining 3 tablespoons of olive oil, and the oregano in a small bowl. Mix them together and set the bowl aside.

To form the flatbread, divide the dough into 14 pieces. Take a piece and roll it into a ball using your palms or using a circular motion on your bench. Then, using your fingers, push the dough out from the center to create a crater in the middle to fill with cheese.

Take 1½ teaspoons of cheese and place it into the dough pocket. Bring the sides of dough together to enclose the cheese inside. Flatten the dough with your palm, and then, on a floured bench, gently push down with a rolling pin. Slowly roll the dough into a circle approximately 10 cm (3.9 in.) in diameter and 1 cm (0.4 in.) thick.

In a pan, heat 3–4 tablespoons of olive oil. Once it is hot, add 1 flatbread at a time, cooking it until it becomes golden brown. Repeat this process on the opposite side. It should take no more than 1–2 minutes on each side. Repeat this process until all the flatbreads are cooked.

These cabbage rolls are unquestionably a warming, wintery dish. Soft cabbage leaves enclose a rice, meat, and herb mixture, and they are finished with a tangy lemon sauce. This recipe can be made a day ahead and slowly reheated, as long as the sauce is added just prior to serving. Cabbage is always abundant through the winter; however, you can use silver beets as an alternative. Just blanch the leaves in salted boiling water for about 3 minutes and then assemble the rolls exactly as the recipe directs below.

Traditionally, this dish is served with *avgolemono* (egg and lemon sauce), but I have altered this somewhat with a sharp lemon sauce that does not use eggs. This dish reminds me of my eldest brother, Bill, who would always call the rolls "Greek sushi."

Cabbage Rolls with Lemon

Lahanodolmades me Lemoni
Λαχανοντολμάδες με Λεμόνι

GLUTEN-FREE
MAKES: 30 PIECES
TIME: 2 HOURS

1 large savoy or wombok (Chinese) cabbage, approximately 2 kg (4.4 lb.)

300 g (8.8 oz./0.66 lb.) minced meat (a combination of veal and pork)

1 large onion, diced

¾ cup finely chopped flat leaf parsley

¾ cup finely chopped mint leaves

¾ cup finely chopped basil leaves

½ cup finely chopped dill

¾ cup medium-grain rice

1 tablespoon salt

½ tablespoon black pepper

½ cup olive oil

Fill a large pot with water, add the salt, and bring the water to a boil. Core the center of the cabbage (if using the savoy variety) and place the cored cabbage into the water. Allow to simmer for approximately 1 hour or until the leaves are soft. Alternatively, if using wombok cabbage, gently undo the leaves (you will need 35 leaves). Drop them in the water in batches, and allow them to simmer for about 30 minutes (wombok cabbage will cook quickly) or until the leaves have softened. Place them into a colander to drain and set them aside. Reserve the water used to boil the leaves.

Line the entire bottom of a casserole dish with cabbage leaves.

In a bowl, place the minced meat, onion, parsley, mint, basil, dill, rice, salt, pepper, and olive oil. Mix the ingredients well. Take a leaf (if using savoy cabbage, cut each leaf in half) and place the stalk end toward you. Place 1 teaspoon of filling on the end closest to you and begin to roll the cabbage away from you, tucking in the sides as you go.

Arrange the cabbage rolls neatly side by side, lining them around the edge of the pan and working your way in. When the bottom of the dish is full, begin a second layer, repeating until you have filled all the cabbage leaves.

Pour enough of the reserved water to just cover the cabbage rolls. Place a medium-size dinner plate (smaller than the circumference of the pot) upside down on top of the rolls to keep them from opening and rising during the cooking. Simmer the rolls over medium heat, partially covered, for about 45 minutes, until the meat and rice are cooked. If there is not enough liquid in the pot, add an extra ½–1 cup of boiled water.

Once the rolls are cooked, pour any remaining liquid into a small pot, being careful that the rolls don't fall out. You will need 1½ cups, so if there is not enough liquid from the cabbage rolls, use the remainder of the reserved water. Add the milk, lemon juice, and corn flour to the water and heat the mixture, whisking constantly until you have a slightly thick sauce. Taste the sauce and season it accordingly. If it is too thick, add a little water or milk to dilute. If a tangier taste is preferred, add the juice of another lemon.

To serve the cabbage rolls, pour the sauce on top and serve with a dollop of Greek yogurt.

LEMON SAUCE

½ cup whole milk

3 lemons, juiced

1½ tablespoons corn flour (corn starch)

Moderation
in all things.
-Terence

Cabbage Rolls with Lemon (page 120)

Potato salad is definitely a classic, one that I ate consistently growing up and one that has endless possibilities. This recipe is unpretentious and easy to prepare. Greeks love potatoes—in more ways than one. Yes, we make dips with them, we fry them in olive oil, we add them to our moussaka, we roast them with our spring lamb, and the list goes on. Though a modest ingredient, potatoes dressed with the simplicity of extra virgin olive oil, lemon juice, and dried oregano taste sublime.

Potatoes can be boiled with the skins on to add a little texture. If you prefer not to sauté the onions, they can be submerged in cold water for 20 minutes to mellow their intensity. Pat them dry and add them to the salad.

Lemon-Dressed Potato Salad

Patatosalata
Πατατοσαλάτα

MAKES: 1-2 SERVINGS
TIME: 45 MINUTES

1 large onion, thinly sliced

¾ cup olive oil, divided

3 medium potatoes

2 tablespoons capers

¼ cup finely chopped flat leaf parsley

½ cup halved Kalamata olives

1 tablespoon dried oregano

1–2 lemons, juiced

Salt, to taste

Black pepper, to taste

1 spring onion, chopped

Sauté the large onion in ¼ cup of the olive oil until the onion is caramelized and soft. Set the onion aside.

Peel the potatoes and cut them into 8 pieces each. Place the potatoes in a pot of salted water and cook them until they are soft but not falling apart. Drain them and set them aside in a bowl. To the potatoes, add the sautéed onions, capers, parsley, and chopped olives. In a separate bowl, whisk together the remaining ½ cup of olive oil, oregano, lemon juice, salt, and pepper. Pour the dressing over the potatoes and gently mix. Scatter the spring onions on top of the salad and serve it immediately.

You can make the salad in advance and dress it just before serving. This potato salad can be eaten cold or warm.

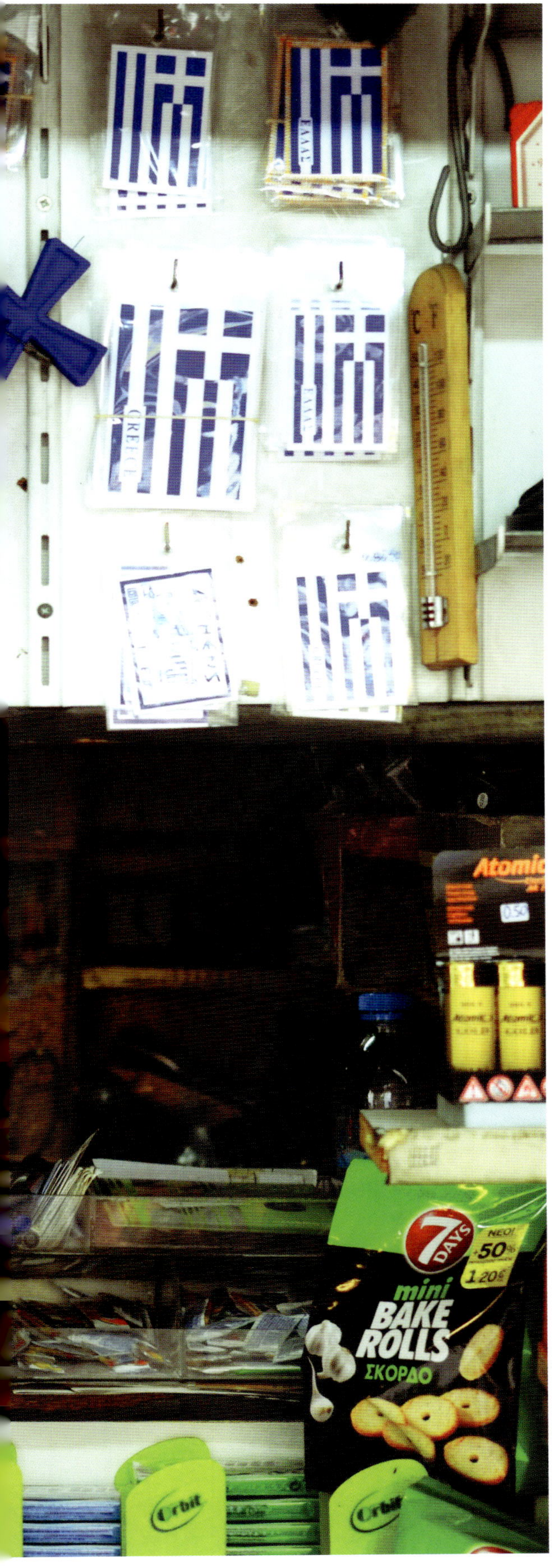
Atomic
0,50
7 DAYS
mini
BAKE ROLLS
ΣΚΟΡΔΟ
Orbit
Orbit

TRAFFIC SISSYS
YHB 7414
YHT 6716

GREECE

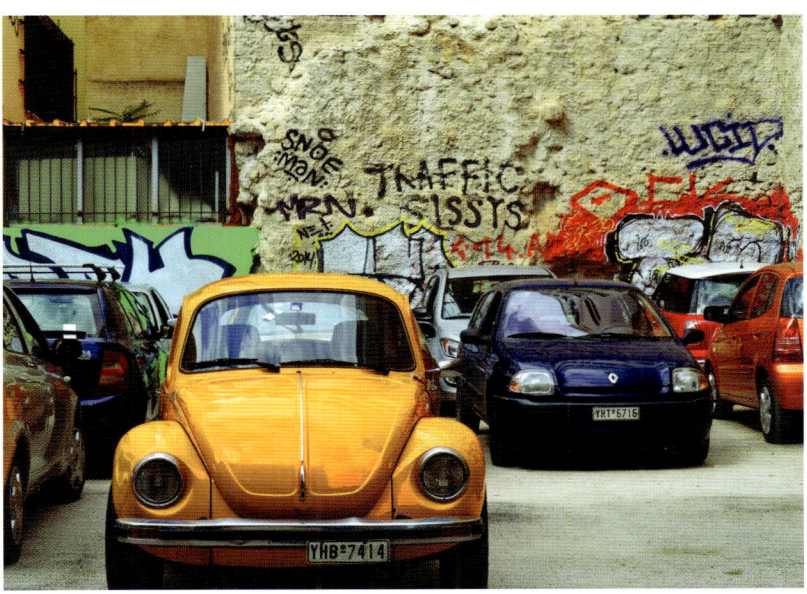

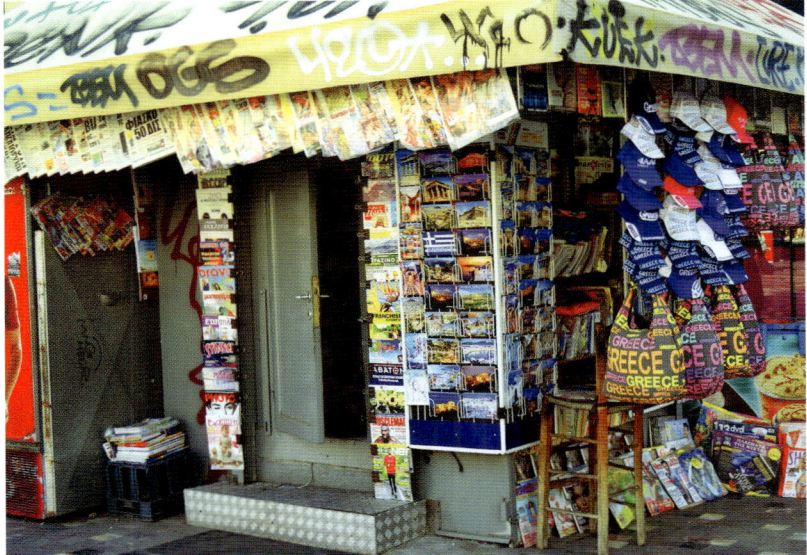

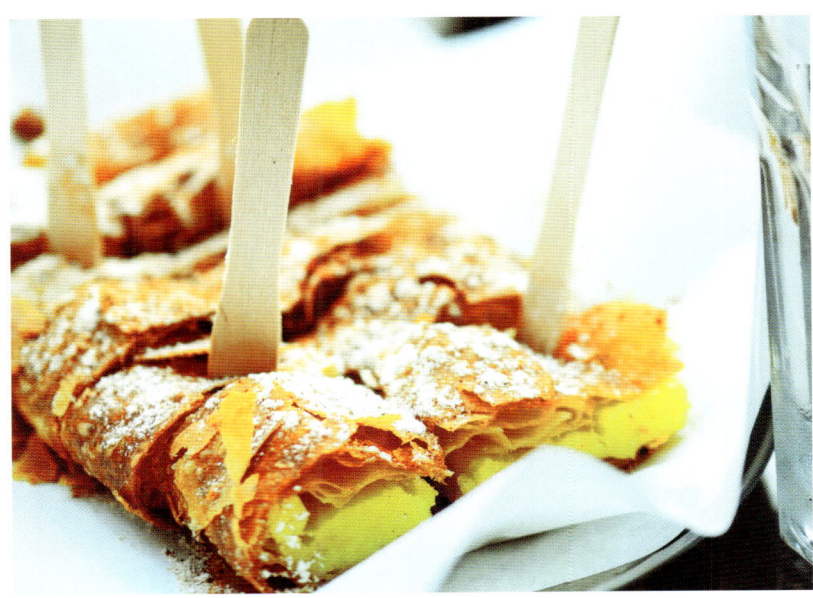

THREE

Baked Foods

Tou Fournou
Του Φούρνου

Homemade Filo Pastry

Cheese Pie

Savory Pumpkin Pie

Spinach Pie

Coiled Spinach Pie

Vegetarian Moussaka (GF)

Little Eggplant Shoes (GF option)

Okra with Lamb and Potatoes (GF)

Stuffed Tomatoes (GF option)

Roasted Baby Goat with Potatoes (GF)

Vegetable Bake (GF)

Pastitsio

Olive Oil and Feta Bread

Cumin Meatballs (GF option)

Squid with Orzo

Ricotta Cheese Pie

Roasted Lamb with Lemon Potatoes (GF)

Egg Meat Loaf

Moussaka (GF option)

Lima Beans Two Ways (GF)

Lazy Housewife Cheese Pie

Stuffed Squid (GF)

Baked Snapper (GF)

GF denotes gluten-free recipes

Baked Foods

"What is that amazing aroma coming from around the corner?" I ask myself as I head toward the fragrance, which is becoming stronger. I find a small but busy bakery filled with the most beautiful pastries and pies. Not merely are they visually tempting, but the aroma is undeniably making me salivate. I gaze upon so many sweet and savory creations: sesame-topped triangles; pastries filled with pumpkin and leek, luscious spinach and wild greens, or savory cheese; syrup-drenched or cinnamon-dusted milk pies; shredded pastry delights; and the list goes on. "If I can buy it, I can make it," I think.

The paper-thin layers of filo pastry are intriguing, and more so when you make the pastry yourself. This method of pastry making petrified me as I watched my grandmother gather flour, oil, salt, and water and make these humble ingredients into a pie. What was born purely from necessity during the difficult days of old has now become a primary staple on our tables. Grandmother would not talk during this process; in a machinelike manner, she would bring together the ingredients—all measurements eyeballed, of course—and knead them into dough, which eventually became a soft, pliable ball. She would let it rest awhile, and then she would take what we call a *plasti* (a thin rolling pin) and slowly roll the dough into a large pizza. As she kept rolling the dough would get thinner and thinner, hardly ever breaking—finally, it would be as big as our dining table. It was an amazing sight. I thought, "If she can do it, I'm sure that if I practice, I can learn."

I played around with various variations and ratios. I watched other elderly Greek ladies, both in Greece and Australia, and looked for ways to improve my method. I failed many times, but that's the way I learned. Finally I grasped what I think is a tasty version. I hope you will not only read the recipe for my Filo Pastry (page 140) but attempt it yourself. Invariably, there will be days the filo works out nicer than others. Without question, there are a few vital things needed when attempting homemade filo. Build up a technique over time, and don't give up after the first attempt. The key ingredients are patience and more patience! You need a large table, plenty of flour (which inevitably will go everywhere in your kitchen and all over your apron), a thin rolling pin, and a joyful attitude. Filo pastry is time consuming, yes, but it's worth every minute.

Pies have their place in a Greek kitchen as feta cheese has its place at every meal. Spanakopita without a doubt is the most common pie associated with Greek cuisine. Wild greens are gathered and then put together with onions, various herbs (both fresh and dry), olive oil, and Greek cheeses. This savory mixture is spread into wonderful filo pastry, drizzled with additional olive oil, and baked. Nutritious and pleasurable!

This chapter is not only about pies but also contains a selection of other foods that are baked.

Γυναίκα που δε θέλει
να ζυμώσει, πέντε
μέρες κοσκινίζει.

Foremost on my agenda when I visit Greece is buying a homemade pie, preferably made with spinach. Pastries are sold all over Greece, so the craving can be fulfilled at any time. Nevertheless, the fun and pleasure of making your own baked goods is incomparable to buying them. Crisp, flaky, thin pastry sheets are an accomplishment attainable once you have the Greek know-how.

This initial recipe, with my few adaptations, has come from Greece. The star is definitely the olive oil. Many pastries use butter as the fat element whereas I have used only olive oil, which adds a great flavor. Filo means "leaf" or "thin paper." To obtain a very thin sheet, use a very thin rolling pin much like a curtain rod. An important tip to remember is to not add all the water to the flour at once. Slowly pour 1 cup at a time and slowly knead the dough until the right consistency is achieved.

Homemade Filo Pastry

Spitiko Filo
Σπιτικό Φύλλο

MAKES: 25 SERVINGS
TIME: 1 HOUR, 30 MINUTES

3 cups all-purpose flour

1½ teaspoons salt

2 tablespoons white or red wine vinegar

½ cup olive oil

1 cup warm water

Corn flour (cornstarch), for dusting

Additional olive oil, for brushing the pastry

Place the flour, salt, vinegar, and oil into a bowl. Slowly add the water, a little at a time, while stirring the ingredients to form dough (you may need another ½ cup of water if it's too dry). Knead the mixture for 5–10 minutes until it all comes together into a very soft dough (add a little extra flour if it is too sticky or a little more water if it is too dry). Cover the dough and allow it to rest for approximately 20 minutes. While the dough is resting, place a baking tray that measures 43 cm by 30 cm (17 in. by 11.8 in.) near your workstation.

Halve the dough and knead each half for about 1 minute. Take 1 piece and roll it out into a thin (½ cm (0.2 in.) or less) large sheet, dusting with corn flour as you go so that it won't stick. (The size of the sheet should preferably be a little larger than the baking tray that will be used.)

Drizzle approximately 6 tablespoons of the olive oil onto the pastry and brush it over the pastry. Start folding and layering the dough by bringing the top and bottom edges to the middle, as if you were folding a letter. Fold over the sides of the dough, brushing oil on each overlay, except the top layer. Wrap the dough in plastic wrap, and place it in the freezer for 10 minutes. Repeat this process with the other half of the pastry. Have both sheets ready before you fill the pie. (This method creates layers of pastry that will separate when baked).

While the pastry is chilling, prepare the filling of your choice (see below). Preheat the oven to 200°C (392°F).

To assemble the pie, dust your work surface with corn flour. Remove 1 pastry from the freezer and slowly roll it out, dusting with corn flour as you go, until it is a little larger than the baking tray. Place the pastry on the bottom of the tray, top it with the filling of your choice, and then fold over any overlaying pastry around the edges. Repeat this process with the top pastry. Gather the filo so that it has no overlay when covering the top (it will have a ruffled effect). With a sharp knife, cut the pie into 25 portions and brush olive oil on top. Place the pie in the refrigerator for 30 minutes before baking (this helps create a crunchier pastry).

Bake the pie for 35 minutes or until it is golden.

Cheese Pie
Τυρόπιτα

2 eggs, whisked together

¾ cup crumbled ricotta cheese

¾ cup crumbled feta cheese

¼ cup olive oil

1 teaspoon salt

1 teaspoon black pepper

Savory Pumpkin Pie
Κολοκυθόπιτα

2 cups grated pumpkin

1½ cups finely chopped leeks

3 spring onions, chopped

2 eggs, whisked together

170 g (¾ cup) crumbled feta cheese

¼ cup olive oil

1 teaspoon salt

1 teaspoon black pepper

Spinach Pie
Σπανακόπιτα

1 cup finely chopped leeks

2 cups chopped raw spinach

3 spring onions, chopped

2 eggs, whisked together

½ cup crumbled feta cheese

¼ cup olive oil

½ cup finely chopped mint

½ cup finely chopped basil

½ cup finely chopped flat leaf parsley

1 teaspoon dried oregano

1 teaspoon salt

1 teaspoon black pepper

Visually appealing, this spiral spinach pie is delicious. It is a crispy and flaky rolled pie stuffed with spinach and feta cheese. I like the simplicity of putting it together. If you exercise a little patience when stretching the dough, before long it will become second nature and a joy to accomplish.

Coiled Spinach Pie

Spanakopita me Strifto Filo
Σπανακόπιτα με Στριφτό Φύλλο

MAKES: 25 SERVINGS
TIME: 2 HOURS

3 cups all-purpose flour

1 tablespoon salt

¼ cup olive oil

1½ cups warm water

Corn flour (cornstarch), for stretching dough

2 cups chopped spinach

½ cup spring onions, chopped

1½ cups crumbled feta cheese

In a bowl, place the flour, salt, and olive oil. Slowly add the water and stir the ingredients until the dough is soft but not sticky (add additional water or flour as required). Place the dough on a lightly floured surface and knead it for approximately 5 minutes or until you have an elastic and soft dough. Allow it to rest for 35 minutes. While the dough is resting, preheat the oven to 200°C (392°F).

Place a large tablecloth on your work surface and dust the tablecloth with corn flour. Halve the dough, placing half aside covered with a cloth. In the meantime, take the other half and place it in the middle of the tablecloth. Sprinkle with a little more corn flour. With a curtain rod or thin rolling pin, start to roll out the dough as large as possible. Brush 5 tablespoons of the olive oil on top of the dough. Leave it 2 minutes and then gently start stretching the dough with your hands until it has opened into a very large and thin filo (a minimum of ½ a meter (19.6 in.) in diameter).

To prepare the filling, place the chopped spinach, spring onions, and feta cheese in a bowl and mix them to combine.

Sprinkle half the filling randomly onto the pastry (it will not look like much, but once the pastry is rolled up, the filling will be plenty). Gently lifting a side of the tablecloth, roll the pastry into a snake shape. Coil the pastry on a baking tray. Repeat this entire process with the other half of the dough. Brush a little olive oil on the top of each pie.

Bake the pie for 30 minutes or until it is golden.

I cannot walk by plump, dark eggplants and not purchase them. They bring an array of dishes to my mind, and I just want to get cooking. We don't associate eggplants with fruit, but they are a fruit and are best eaten in summer. This recipe is a vegetarian version of the traditional moussaka. It makes use of the abundance of Greek vegetables. It has three main components: the gluten-free white sauce, the mushroom sauce, and the vegetable layers (the surprise ingredient is the feta cheese). This moussaka can be made a day in advance and be refrigerated.

Vegetarian Moussaka

Moussaka Lahanikon
Μουσακάς Λαχανικών

GLUTEN-FREE
MAKES: 9 SERVINGS
TIME: 2 HOURS, 30 MINUTES

MUSHROOM SAUCE

½ cup olive oil

1 large onion, sliced

500 g (17.6 oz./1.1 lb.) sliced button mushrooms

1½ cups tomato puree

½ cup water

Salt, to taste

Black pepper, to taste

½ teaspoon castor (superfine) sugar

VEGETABLE LAYER

4 red capsicums (bell peppers), roasted and peeled*

1 large eggplant, sliced lengthwise into ½ cm (0.2 in.) discs

3 zucchinis (courgettes), sliced lengthwise into ½ cm (0.2 in.) strips

4 potatoes, peeled and sliced into ½ cm (0.2 in.) discs

Light olive oil, for frying

Preheat the oven to 210°C (410°F).

To prepare the mushroom sauce, sauté the onion in the olive oil until the onion is soft. Add the mushrooms, tomato puree, water, salt, pepper, and sugar and allow the mixture to simmer over low heat for 20 minutes or until the mushrooms have wilted down and the sauce is thick. Do not allow the sauce to dry out too much—you need a thick sauce to moisten the vegetable bake. If it looks too dry, add ½ cup of water. Once the mushroom sauce has thickened, set it aside.

Place the red capsicums on a tray and bake them until they are blistered and soft. (If you are using jarred roasted capsicums, skip this step.) Remove them from oven; when they have cooled, peel the skins off. Set the roasted capsicums aside.

Heat 3 tablespoons of olive oil in a shallow frying pan over medium-high heat. Season the eggplant and zucchini with salt and pepper. Fry the eggplant slices in batches, adding a few tablespoons of oil to the pan if they start to stick, until they are light golden brown on both sides. Repeat this process with the zucchinis. Place everything on a paper towel to drain any excess oil.

Fill a shallow frying pan ¼ full of olive oil; when the oil is hot, fry the potatoes until they are golden brown. Drain them and set them aside.

To make the white sauce, dilute the corn flour in a small bowl with the water. Set this mixture aside.

In a saucepan, add the milk, egg, nutmeg, and salt. Whisk the mixture to break up the egg, and then heat it until it is hot but not boiling. Slowly pour in the corn flour, continuously whisking the sauce for about 10 minutes or until it has thickened (usually at the boiling point). Take the pan off the heat and taste the sauce for seasoning, adjusting it if needed.

To assemble the moussaka, drizzle some olive oil on the bottom of a large baking dish (34 cm by 24 cm by 5 cm/13.3 in. by 9.4 in. by 2 in.). Layer the potatoes in the bottom of the dish and sprinkle them with 1 tablespoon of kefalotiri cheese. On top of the potatoes, layer the zucchini and sprinkle it with 1 tablespoon of kefalotiri cheese. On top of the zucchini, layer the eggplant and sprinkle it with 1 tablespoon of kefalotiri cheese. On top of the eggplant, layer the roasted capsicums. Scatter the crumbled feta cheese over the capsicums and top that with the mushroom sauce. Top the mushroom sauce with the white sauce, and then add the remaining cheese.

Bake the moussaka for 1 hour or until it is golden brown. Allow it to cool for 10 minutes and serve it with a Greek salad.

—

Ready-roasted capsicums are also sold in jars at most supermarkets and can be used as a substitute.

†*Kefalotiri cheese can be substituted with Parmesan cheese.*

GLUTEN-FREE WHITE SAUCE

60 g (2.1 oz. / 0.13 lb.) corn flour (cornstarch)

¼ cup water

4 cups whole milk

1 egg

½ tablespoon grated nutmeg

Salt, to taste

70 g (2.4 oz./0.1 lb.) grated kefalotiri cheese†

125 g (4 oz./0.27 lb.) feta cheese, crumbled

This dish has flavors similar to moussaka; however, unlike moussaka, it has been deconstructed into individual portions. This dish gets its name from the resemblance of the eggplant to little shoes. I bake the eggplant on a tasty base of tomato sauce. Traditionally, white sauce is poured on the top, but I substitute a generous helping of yellow cheese instead. As an alternative to the minced beef bolognaise-style stuffing, I have substituted meatballs placed on top of the eggplant.

Little Eggplant Shoes

Papoutsakia
Παπουτσάκια

GLUTEN-FREE*
MAKES: 6 SERVINGS
TIME: 2 HOURS

3 medium eggplants, cut in half and each drizzled with 1 tablespoon olive oil

MEAT STUFFING

500 g (17.6 oz. /1.1 lb.) minced beef

3 garlic cloves, minced

1 onion, diced and sautéed in ¼ cup olive oil

1 egg

¼ cup finely chopped flat leaf parsley

½ cup finely chopped mint

½ cup bread crumbs*

1 teaspoon mild paprika

1 teaspoon black pepper

1 teaspoon dried oregano

1 teaspoon cumin powder

¾ tablespoon salt

¼ cup olive oil

Preheat the oven to 210°C (410°F).

With a small paring knife, make crisscross incisions in the flesh of the eggplant halves. Season them with salt and drizzle them with a little olive oil. Place them in a baking dish and bake them 30–40 minutes or until the eggplant skin is soft and the inside flesh is juicy and golden. With a fork, remove some of the flesh so that the meatball will fit snugly in the eggplant.

Add all the meatball ingredients into a bowl and mix well using your hands. Divide the mixture into 6 portions and roll each into an oval-shaped ball to fit perfectly on top of each eggplant half. Place 1 on each eggplant. Set aside until the sauce is made.

To make the tomato sauce, place the onion and olive oil in a pan. Sauté the onion until it is soft. Add the remaining ingredients to the pan and cook over medium heat for 10 minutes. Pour the mixture into a deep baking dish (30 cm by 22 cm by 5 cm/11 in. by 8.6 in. by 2 in.). Place the eggplant halves carefully onto the sauce side by side.

Bake them for 40 minutes. Remove them from the oven and gently turn the meatballs over (not the eggplant) so that they cook on both sides. Return to the oven and bake them for an additional 20 minutes or until the meat is golden.

> Beware the barrenness
> of a busy life.
> -Socrates

Remove the eggplants from the oven and place cheese on each eggplant. Bake for an additional 10 minutes or until the cheese is golden brown.

Serve this dish with mashed potatoes and a spoonful of the sauce.

—

For a gluten-free option, replace the bread crumbs with 1 grated potato (be sure to squeeze out excess water).

†*Kefalograviera cheese can be substituted with any hard yellow cheese.*

SAUCE

1 onion, diced

½ cup olive oil

440 ml (14.8 fl oz.) tomato puree

1 cup water

1 bay leaf

2 teaspoons cumin

½ tablespoon salt

150 g (5.2 oz./0.33 lb.) kefalograviera cheese slices† for topping

Little Eggplant Shoes
(page 146)

I was possibly the most peculiar child when it came to okra. No child I ever knew liked this "slimy vegetable," as we called it, except for me. There were certain dishes I shunned as a child, but this one, being the most unusual, was a favorite of mine. I would plead with Mum to cook it for me. Now, as an adult, I find myself cooking it very regularly and having fun with various recipes, both with and without meat.

Okra is a green vegetable best eaten during the summer months, when it is fresh and in season. Okra is high in antioxidants, calcium, and potassium. It is a delicious vegetable that needs to be cooked appropriately; otherwise, it can have a very slimy consistency in the pod. Okra is generally cooked using plenty of olive oil and tomatoes.

Okra with Lamb and Potatoes

Bamies me Arnaki
Μπάμιες με Αρνάκι

GLUTEN-FREE
MAKES: 4-6 SERVINGS
TIME: 1 HOUR, 30 MINUTES-2 HOURS

450 g (15.8 oz./1 lb.) fresh okra

½ cup red wine vinegar

½ cup olive oil

1 large onion, thinly sliced

500 g (17.6 oz./1.1 lb.) lamb rump or chops (omit this for a vegetarian version)

Salt, to taste

Black pepper, to taste

2 garlic cloves, sliced

1 cinnamon quill

1 teaspoon mild paprika

1 teaspoon dried oregano

4 large tomatoes, skinned and grated

1 cup tomato puree

2 medium potatoes, quartered

1 cup water

Preheat the oven to 220°C (428°F).

Wash the okra. Using a paring knife, gently peel around the head of the okra, ensuring you do not totally cut it off. You want to remove only the outer layer of the pointed end.

Dip the pointed ends of the okra pods into the vinegar and set them aside. This will ensure that the seeds stay intact.

Heat the olive oil on the stove in an oven-safe pan, adding the sliced onion and allowing the onion to soften for a few minutes. Add the lamb and season it with salt and pepper. Brown the meat well on all sides, and then add the garlic and okra. Sauté this mixture for 5 minutes and then add the remaining ingredients, ensuring that the liquid is covering the okra (if it is not, add another 2 grated tomatoes and a little additional water). Cover and cook over medium heat for 30 minutes, and then place the pan in the oven uncovered for 40 minutes or until the okra is soft, the potatoes are cooked through, and the olive oil has come to the surface. Serve the okra with crusty bread (gluten-free, if desired).

Gemista means "stuffed." Whenever my mum would see plump, ripe tomatoes at the fruit market, she would always buy fifteen to twenty of them and effortlessly begin the process of collecting all the herbs and spices she would need to fill two huge baking trays of stuffed tomatoes. Our drive home always included a detour along a rural road that had organic herbs by the wayside or a stop at a relative's garden to collect a large amount of fresh dill. This was a task Mum undertook without fretting, completing it with joy and love. I find myself doing the same thing as an adult.

Stuffed tomatoes bring back memories of many people eating and enjoying each other's company. Each time I make them, I like to have company—and plenty of it. It is a satisfying vegetarian meal that feeds a crowd. Don't withhold the olive oil here. While it seems like a lot, it is the reason why this dish tastes so good. For my mum's meat-filled version, add 250 g (8.8 oz.) of minced beef to the mixture before stuffing the vegetables.

Stuffed Tomatoes

Domates Gemistes
Ντομάτες Γεμιστές

GLUTEN-FREE
MAKES: 5 SERVINGS
<2 PER PERSON>
TIME: 1 HOUR, 30 MINUTES - 2 HOURS

Preheat the oven to 210°C (410°F).

Wash the tomatoes. Slice off the top of the tomatoes and scoop out the flesh. Place the flesh into a food processor, blend it, and set it aside. Put the tomatoes in a baking dish and season the insides with a pinch of salt.

Sauté the onions and garlic in ⅓ of the olive oil until they are soft. Add the blended tomato and cook the mixture for about 6 minutes. Pour this mixture into a large bowl and add the rice, parsley, mint, dill, oregano, tomato paste, ketchup, salt, and pepper. Mix the ingredients well and taste it to ensure it is well seasoned.

Spoon this mixture into the tomatoes. Place the quartered potatoes between the tomatoes. Combine tomato puree and 1 cup of water in a bowl. Mix well and pour around the tomatoes. Pour in the remaining olive oil and sprinkle breadcrumbs over the top. Bake, uncovered, for approximately 1½ hours. The juices will evaporate by half, and a lovely layer of oil will be sitting at the bottom of the pan.

Serve the stuffed tomatoes with feta cheese and olives. If you have leftovers, they are just as wonderful the next day.

—

Make-ahead tip: Wash the tomatoes and scoop out the insides 1 day prior to baking. Arrange them in a baking dish, cover the dish with plastic wrap, and refrigerate the tomatoes until you are ready to fill them.

10 medium ripe tomatoes

1½ cups olive oil

2 large onions, diced

2 garlic cloves, chopped

1 cup medium-grain rice

½ cup finely chopped flat leaf parsley

½ cup finely chopped mint

½ cup finely chopped dill

1 tablespoon dried oregano

2 tablespoons tomato paste

1 tablespoon tomato ketchup

1½ teaspoon salt

1½ teaspoon black pepper

2 large potatoes, peeled and quartered

1 cup tomato puree

1 cup water

¼ cup fresh bread crumbs (omit for a gluten-free version)

Goat meat is considered nutritious because of its low fat content and because it is easy to digest. This dish reminds me of my father-in-law. For a time, my husband and I would go weekly to his home for some hearty, slow-cooked goat. He would cook it on the stove and serve it with Greek pasta. It is a tradition in my in-laws' home.

I have adapted this recipe and chosen to bake the goat instead, which gives it a lovely charred taste. It's a great dish, easy to prepare, and uses only one pot. It is lovely to place the dish in the center of the table and watch as family members and guests all help themselves. Serve with a dollop of tzatziki and crusty homemade (or gluten-free) bread.

Roasted Baby Goat with Potatoes

Katsikaki me Patates
Κατσικάκι με Πατάτες

GLUTEN-FREE
MAKES: 5-6 SERVINGS
TIME: 2 HOURS, 25 MINUTES

1 kg (35.2 oz. /2.2 lb.) baby goat, cut into 3 cm (1.2 in.) pieces

¾ cup olive oil

6 tomatoes, quartered

2 onions, sliced

2 whole garlic cloves, sliced

2 cups water

2 teaspoons dried oregano

2 teaspoons mild paprika

2 sprigs fresh rosemary

3 sprigs fresh Greek oregano

1 tablespoon salt

1 teaspoon black pepper

6 large potatoes, peeled and quartered

Preheat the oven to 240°C (464°F).

Place all the ingredients (except the potatoes) in an ovenproof baking dish. Mix to combine. Cover the dish and bake the goat for 1½ hours. Remove the dish from the oven and add the potatoes, mixing well to coat them with the juices from the pan. Sprinkle some extra salt on top, cover the dish again, and bake for another 30 minutes.

Uncover the dish and replace in the oven, allowing the food to brown for about 25 minutes or until the potatoes are completely cooked through and golden. Serve the dish immediately.

Briam, the traditional name for this dish, comes from Turkey; however, the singsong Greek name *Tourlou Tourlou* refers to a peasant dish or, more precisely, a medley of vegetables. Generously coated with olive oil, the seasonal vegetables are roasted, releasing an intense sweetness. The keys to this recipe are low heat and slow cooking time. Always serve this recipe with feta cheese and bread (or gluten-free bread). And, most importantly, mop up the juices from the pan—they are by far the best part of this dish! A humble, healthy, and delightful summer dish, this can be eaten hot or even at room temperature the next day.

Vegetable Bake

Briam or Tourlou
Μπριάμ ή Τουρλού

GLUTEN-FREE
MAKES: 4–5 SERVINGS
PREP: 15 MINUTES
TIME: 1 HOUR, 30 MINUTES

Preheat the oven to 220°C (428°F).

Add all the ingredients to a large baking dish, mixing them well. Bake, covered, for approximately 30 minutes. Uncover the dish and bake the vegetables for another 40–50 minutes or until the vegetables are cooked, the water has evaporated by half, and the olive oil has risen to the top. Allow the vegetables to cool slightly before serving. Serve with feta cheese and crusty bread.

—

Tip: The key to a great vegetable bake is to cut all the vegetables into pieces that are relatively the same size and to bake them as long as possible, ensuring the water has evaporated.

- 4 medium potatoes, sliced into 1 cm (½ in.) rounds
- 1 large eggplant, sliced into 1 cm (½ in.) rounds
- 3 small zucchinis (courgettes), sliced into 1 cm (½ in.) rounds
- 2 large onions, sliced into 1 cm (½ in.) rounds
- 1 red capsicum (bell pepper), sliced
- 750 g (26.4 oz./1.6 lb.) tomatoes, grated
- 6 garlic cloves
- ½ cup finely chopped flat leaf parsley
- ½ cup finely chopped mint
- 1 cup olive oil
- 2 teaspoons dried oregano
- 1 tablespoon tomato paste
- ½ cup tomato puree
- 1 cup water
- Salt, to taste
- Black pepper, to taste

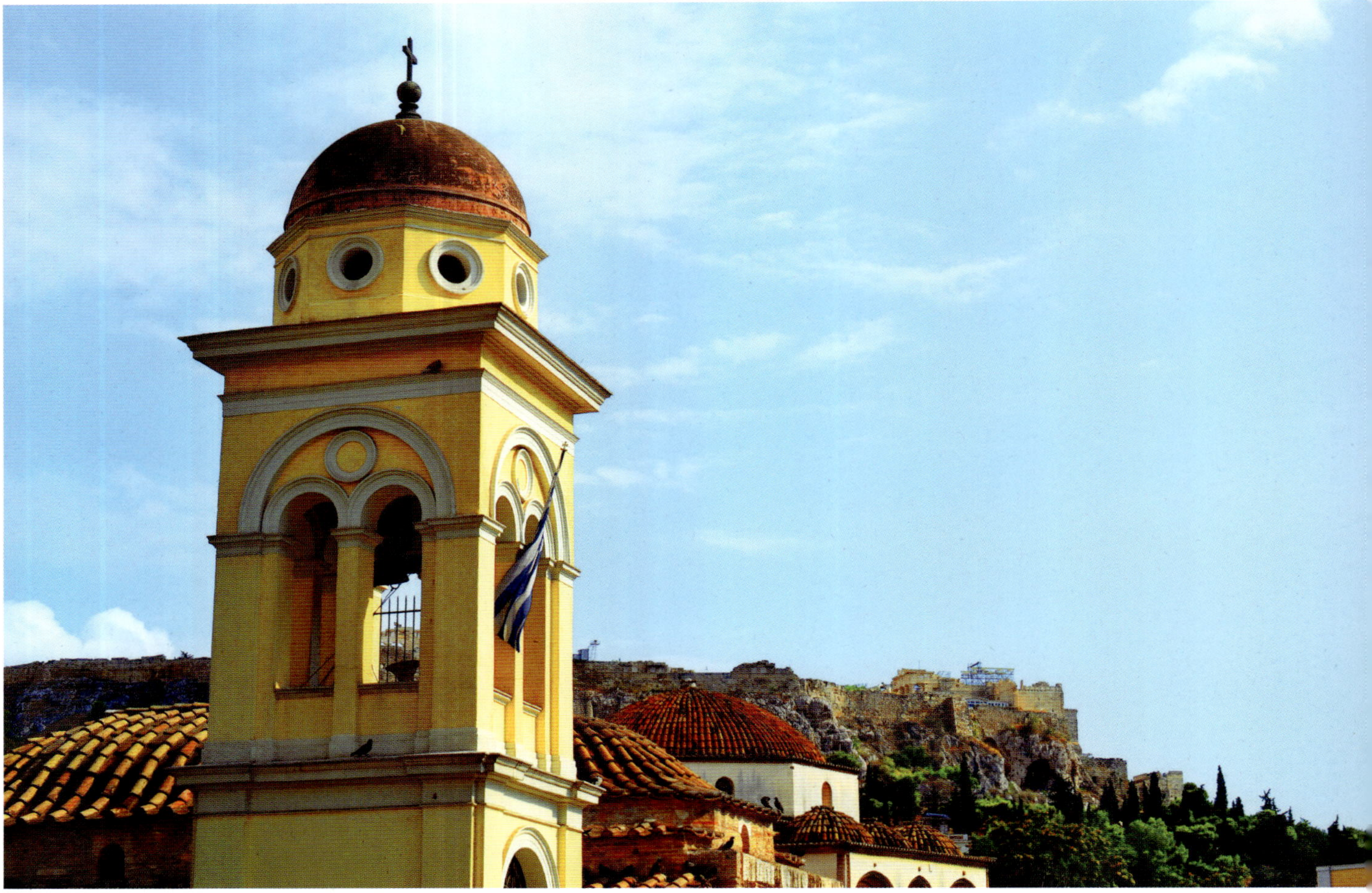

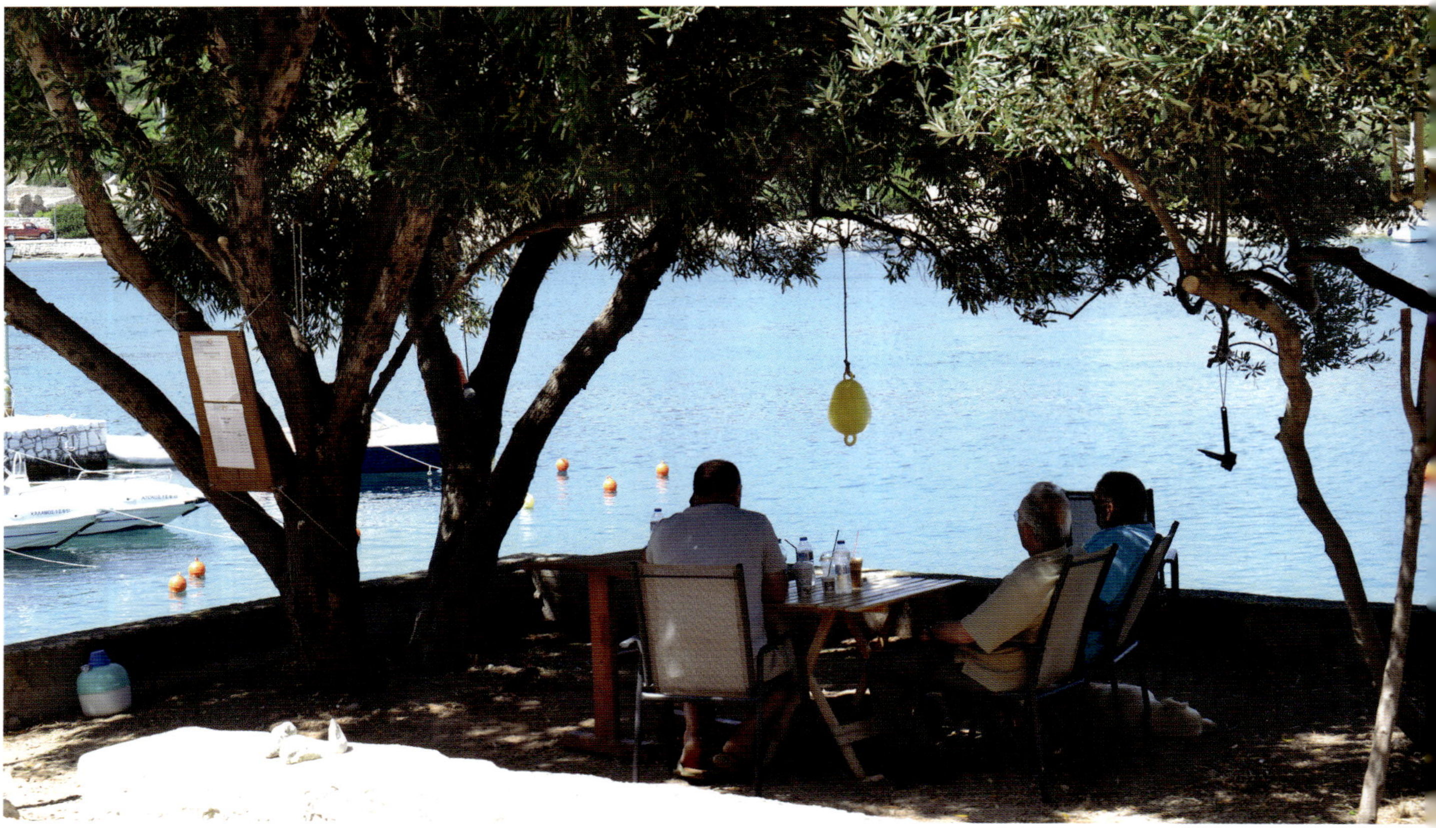

Pastitsio (page 158)

Pastitsio is to Greeks what lasagna is to Italians. It is a dish suited for a celebration: pasta hidden beneath cinnamon-spiced meat and a creamy white sauce. Pastitsio is generally made with thick, tubular pasta, but I prefer spaghetti. Ideally, pastitsio is best eaten about twenty minutes after it has been removed from the oven. You do not want it piping hot. This also helps the pastitsio to set somewhat, so that when you slice the portions, the pastitsio won't collapse. Three layers make one amazing dish. This is one of those dishes that will please the smallest to the largest crowd.

MAKES: 12 SERVINGS
TIME: 2 HOURS

MEAT SAUCE

½ cup olive oil

3 garlic cloves, minced

500 g (17.6 oz. /1.1 lb.) minced beef

2 teaspoons salt

1 teaspoon black pepper

1 teaspoon mild paprika

2 teaspoons cinnamon powder

¼ teaspoon ground cloves

6 whole cloves

1 cinnamon quill

1 bay leaf

3 tablespoons tomato paste

2 cups tomato puree

1 cup red wine

2 cups water

2 teaspoons castor (superfine) sugar

500 g (16 oz. /1.1 lb.) spaghetti

½ cup grated kefalograviera cheese*

Pastitsio

Pastitsio
Παστίτσιο

To prepare the meat sauce, heat the oil with the garlic in a medium pan over medium heat. Sauté the garlic until it starts to sizzle, being careful not to burn it. Add the beef and start to break it up using a wooden spoon, allowing it to brown well. Do not hurry this step—it is crucial to take it slowly. Brown the meat until all the juices have evaporated and the oil has come to the surface. Add the salt and spices to the beef. Cook for 1 minute and then add the tomato paste, cooking for another 3 minutes. Add the tomato puree, wine, water, and sugar. Simmer the sauce over low heat, covered, for approximately 35–40 minutes, until the meat is cooked, the sauce has reduced, and the oil has come to the surface. Set the sauce aside.

Preheat the oven to 220°C (428°F).

Cook the spaghetti in boiling, salted water. Drain the pasta and transfer it to a baking dish (34 cm by 24 cm by 5 cm/13.3 in. by 9.4 in. by 2 in.). Liberally sprinkle the grated cheese over the top of the pasta and stir it well. Pour the meat sauce on top of the pasta.

To make the white sauce, place the flour in a bowl with the water to create a runny batter, whisking it to remove any lumps. In a pot, add the milk and the whisked egg, mixing them well to combine. Add the salt. Heat the milk, and then add the flour batter, whisking continuously to remove any lumps until the sauce thickens. This should take about 10 minutes or until the sauce reaches the boiling point.

Take the white sauce off the stove and add the grated nutmeg and the cheese. Pour the sauce on top of the meat and sprinkle the sugar, bread crumbs, and the extra ¼ cup cheese over the casserole.

Bake the pastitsio for 45 minutes or until it is golden on top. Allow the dish to cool down for 15–20 minutes before serving it. Pastitsio is best eaten with a Greek salad and tzatziki.

—

Kefalograviera is a Greek cheese that can be purchased from any international delicatessen. Use parmesan cheese as a substitute, if necessary.

Make-ahead tip: Prepare the meat sauce and the pasta 1 day in advance. Assemble the casserole in the baking dish, cover it, and refrigerate it until it's needed. The following day, make the white sauce and bake the casserole according to the directions above.

WHITE SAUCE

1½ cups all-purpose flour

1½ cups water

1 L (33.8 fl. oz.) whole milk

1 egg whisked

Salt, to taste

1 teaspoon freshly grated nutmeg

200 g (7 oz./0.44 lb.) grated kefalograviera cheese, plus ¼ cup extra for topping

2 teaspoons castor (superfine) sugar

¼ cup bread crumbs

1 teaspoon salt

My father-in-law's response after having eaten this bread was, "My mother used to make a bread very similar to this over sixty years ago." Now, this is the reaction I'm looking for as people eat my food: the joy of memories engraved in one's childhood. This recipe is humble yet pleasurable to eat, reminding us of the simplicity of olive oil and feta cheese. No kneading is required; rather, it's a wet batter that gets poured into a baking tray, and off it goes. As it bakes, the house starts to smell like a Greek bakery. The feta cheese starts to brown, and the oregano releases an amazing aroma. It is a cross between a bread loaf and a focaccia. You can sprinkle coarse salt on top or even add some rosemary before baking.

Olive Oil and Feta Bread

Kourkoutopita
Κουρκουτόπιτα

MAKES: 6-8 SERVINGS
TIME: 1 HOUR, 10 MINUTES

2 tablespoons dry instant yeast

2 cups lukewarm water

3 cups all-purpose flour

300 g (10.5 oz./0.66 lb.) crumbled feta cheese

½ cup olive oil

1 tablespoon dried oregano

1 teaspoon salt

TOPPING

100 g (3.5 oz./0.22 lb.) crumbled feta cheese

½ tablespoon dried oregano

¼ cup olive oil

Preheat the oven to 210°C (410°F).

Place all the dough ingredients into a large bowl and mix them with a wooden spoon. This will be a wet and sticky dough. Allow the dough to stand for 10 minutes, covered with a cloth.

Oil a baking tray roughly 28 cm by 22 cm (11 in. by 8.6 in.). Note that if you choose a smaller tray, the bread will be higher; alternatively, a longer pan will make a narrower bread more like a focaccia.

Place the oiled tray into the oven and heat it for 10 minutes.

Remove the tray from the oven and transfer the dough to the tray without stirring it. Gently push down on the dough with a wooden spoon so that it covers the whole tray. Sprinkle the top with feta cheese and oregano, and then drizzle it with olive oil. Bake the bread for approximately 40 minutes or until it is golden and cooked through.

The origins of this dish lie in Smyrna, or modern-day Izmir; however, Greeks have embraced it as one of their most traditional foods. No need to get hung up on the Turkish-Greek debate—just enjoy! These cumin-spiced meatballs are added to a delicious tomato sauce and served with white rice.

Cumin Meatballs

Soutzoukakia
Σουτζουκάκια

GLUTEN-FREE*
MAKES: 20 MEATBALLS
TIME: 1 HOUR, 25 MINUTES

MEATBALLS

1 large onion, diced

¼ cup olive oil

2 slices of bread,* crusts removed

1 cup whole milk

250 g minced beef (8.8 oz./0.55 lb.)

250 g minced lamb (8.8 oz./0.55 lb.)

2 garlic cloves, minced

1 tablespoon red wine vinegar

1 egg

½ teaspoon fennel seeds

1½ teaspoons cumin

½ teaspoon paprika

½ tablespoon salt

½ tablespoon black pepper

½ cup finely chopped flat leaf parsley

½ cup finely chopped mint

SAUCE

1 onion, diced

2 garlic cloves, minced

½ cup olive oil

1 bay leaf

1 teaspoon castor (superfine) sugar

Salt, to taste

Black pepper, to taste

2 cups tomato puree

1 cup water

Preheat the oven to 220°C (428°F).

To prepare the meatballs, sauté the onion with the olive oil until the onion is soft and translucent. Set the onion aside to cool.

Chop the bread into bite-size pieces and put them into a small bowl along with the milk. Allow the bread to soak up the milk for about 5 minutes, and then scoop the bread out with your hands, squeezing out any excess liquid. Discard the remaining milk.

Place the soaked bread into a bowl with all the remaining meatball ingredients, including the cooled cooked onion. Mix everything together with your hands and make oval shaped balls a little larger than the size of a golf ball. Place the meatballs on a baking tray and bake them for 35 minutes or until they are browned and cooked through ¾ of the way. Remove them from the oven and set them aside.

To prepare the sauce, sauté the onion and garlic in the olive oil until they are soft. Add all the remaining ingredients and cook over low to medium heat for 15 minutes or until the sauce is thick and glossy. Taste the sauce and adjust the seasoning if needed. To the cooked sauce, add the meatballs and allow everything to heat through for about 10 minutes. Serve with plain white rice.

—

*Omit the slices of bread for a gluten-free option.

Giouvetsi is a hearty, slow-cooked aromatic stew that is generally made with red meat and cooked in clay pots. The stew is braised for hours, and orzo pasta (*kritharaki*) is added during the last half hour of cooking. The pasta cooks and takes on the beautiful flavors of the spices in the stew. To complete the dish, a generous sprinkling of Greek mizithra cheese is added. My recipe uses the same technique and spices but substitutes squid for the red meat. Credit for this recipe goes to my fisherman father-in-law.

Squid with Orzo

Giouvetsi Kalamaraki
Γιουβέτσι Καλαμαράκι

MAKES: 6-8 SERVINGS
TIME: 1 HOUR, 30 MINUTES

½ cup olive oil

2 garlic cloves, minced

1 small onion, chopped

750 g (26.5 oz. / 1.6 lb.) squid, cut into bite-size pieces

2 cups red wine

500 g (16.9 fl oz. / 1.1 lb.) tomato puree

1 tablespoon tomato paste

1 teaspoon cinnamon

Salt, to taste

1 teaspoon black pepper

1½ cups orzo pasta

Preheat the oven to 210°C (410°F).

In a saucepan, sauté the onion and garlic in olive oil until they are soft. Add the squid and the wine. Cook the mixture, uncovered, for about 15 minutes or until the squid has softened and changed color slightly.

Pour the squid mixture into a baking dish. Add the tomato puree, tomato paste, cinnamon, salt, pepper, orzo, and 4 cups of boiled water to the dish, mixing everything together.

Bake the squid for around 50 minutes or until the water has nearly evaporated and the orzo pasta is fully cooked through. You may need to add a little more boiled water if it seems to be drying out during the cooking.

Serve hot with mizithra* cheese.

—

*Mizithra cheese available at international delicatessens.

This cheese pie is made using store-bought pastry, and I make no apology for it. There are great commercial pastries that work very well for particular recipes, and this is one of them. This recipe calls for soda water, which helps create a crisp filo topping. This pastry is very delicate and dries out very quickly, so you must work fast or, alternatively, cover the pastry with a damp cloth. This pie can be eaten cold or hot.

Ricotta Cheese Pie

Anthotiropita
Ανθοτυρόπιτα

MAKES: 8 SERVINGS
TIME: 40 MINUTES

½ cup olive oil

250 g (8.8 oz./0.55 lb.) feta cheese, crumbled

500 g (17.6 oz./1.1 lb.) ricotta (or cottage) cheese

1 cup soda water

4 eggs

450 g (15 oz.) filo pastry

2 tablespoons sesame seeds

Preheat the oven to 190°C (374°F).

Oil a circular 25 cm by 25 cm (9.8 in) oven dish.

Combine the oil, feta cheese, ricotta (or cottage) cheese, soda water, and eggs. Mix these together well and set the mixture aside.

Take 1 sheet of filo pastry and gather it into pleats. Pick it up, and place it into your baking dish. Repeat this process with the remaining filo sheets until the baking tray is full.

Slowly ladle spoonsful of the cheese mixture all around, trying to get the mixture between the layers of filo. Sprinkle the sesame seeds on top, and bake the pie for about 20 minutes or until it is golden brown.

Serve warm.

Food and tradition are embedded and liberally displayed in Greek life. However, the most sacred tradition is Holy Week, during Easter. Meticulous effort is made to season and prepare the lamb feast to be eaten on Easter Sunday. A whole, succulent lamb is skewered on a rotisserie and spiced with garlic, rosemary, lemon, and olive oil. The lamb cooks slowly over hot coals, being rotated for six to eight hours, until the moist, tender meat is literally falling off the bone. A Sunday roast at home, using a leg of lamb infused with the same spices and served with lemon potatoes, is the closest you can get to that delicious Easter meal.

Jesus is depicted as the Lamb that was slain for our sins. The Bible clearly reveals that these rituals, though enjoyable, are not what give us freedom from sin. There is only one way for sins to be forgiven, and that is believing in Jesus as the glorious Lamb of God. Jesus said, "Unless you believe that I am he you will die in your sins" (John 8:24). "The blood of Jesus [God's Son] cleanses us from all sin" (1 John 1:7).

Roasted Lamb with Lemon Potatoes

Arni Sto Fourno me Lemonates Patates
Αρνί Στο Φούρνο με Λεμονάτες Πατάτες

GLUTEN-FREE
MAKES: 6 SERVINGS
TIME: 3 HOURS, 15 MINUTES

ROASTED LAMB

1 lamb shoulder or leg

10 sprigs fresh rosemary, 2 cm (1 in.)

8 garlic cloves, quartered

¼ cup olive oil

2 teaspoons dried oregano

Salt, to taste

Black pepper, to taste

LEMON POTATOES

6 potatoes, peeled and quartered

2 lemons, juiced

1 tablespoon dried oregano

¼ cup olive oil

Salt, to taste

Black pepper, to taste

Preheat the oven to 240°C (464°F).

To prepare the lamb, make random incisions about 2 cm (1 in.) deep in the lamb with a sharp knife. Insert a piece of garlic and rosemary into each slit. Rub the lamb with olive oil. Sprinkle the meat with oregano, salt, and pepper. Place the lamb in a roasting tray with 2½ cups of water. Cover the roast and bake it for 2 hours.

Remove the roast from the oven and arrange the potatoes around the lamb. Add the lemon juice, oregano, olive oil, salt, and pepper. Reduce the heat to 210°C (410°F) and cook, uncovered, for an additional 40 minutes or until the potatoes are soft and golden and the lamb is cooked through. Remove the roast from oven and allow it to rest for 10 minutes. Carve the lamb and serve the dish with a Greek salad.

My father-in-law, Greece 1980

Pleasure in the job puts perfection in the work.
—Aristotle

Egg Meat Loaf (page 172)

This meal is elegant and attractive as well as comforting. It reminds me of a high-end hamburger that needs to eaten with a knife and fork. As you slice into it, a slight crunching sound from the salty prosciutto begins, and then the eggs are revealed with their bright yellow yolks. Although this dish is traditionally made by rolling minced meat into a log shape (hence the name *rolo* meaning "rolled"), I have opted to use a baking tin, as the meat loaf will emerge more uniform in shape and thus more decorative. When I prepared this for my mum recently, the first words that proceeded from her mouth were, "It tastes like the one I used to make when you were a child." That makes me want to cry in sentiment. When a recipe is handed down, and the next generation can produce it without any specific measurements or recipe, it's quite impressive. Praise goes to my mum for having me by her side so I could watch every step and everything she did. Little did I realize that I was learning how to cook just like her!

Egg Meat Loaf

Rolo me Avga
Ρολό με Αυγά

MAKES: 6 SERVINGS
TIME: 2 HOURS

MEAT LOAF

5 eggs

¼ cup olive oil

1 large onion, finely chopped

2 garlic cloves, minced

750 g (26.4 oz./1.6 lb.) minced beef

1 egg

½ cup finely chopped flat leaf parsley

½ cup finely chopped mint

2 cups bread crumbs

½ cup olive oil

1 teaspoon cumin

1 teaspoon mild paprika

1 tablespoon salt

1 teaspoon black pepper

1 tablespoon dried oregano

15 slices prosciutto

Preheat the oven to 220°C (428°F).

Place the 5 eggs into a saucepan and cover them with water. Bring to a boil and simmer for 10 minutes. Drain the pot and set the eggs aside to cool. When the eggs are cold enough to handle, peel off the shells; Dust the peeled eggs in a little flour and set aside.

In a sauté pan, add the olive oil and sauté the onion and garlic until they are soft and translucent. Set them aside to cool. In a large bowl, add the meat, egg, parsley, mint, bread crumbs, olive oil, cumin, paprika, salt, pepper, dried oregano, and cooled onion and garlic mixture. Mix the ingredients gently with your hands to incorporate.

Oil a loaf tin that measures 30 cm by 12 cm by 6 cm (12 in. by 4.5 in. by 2.5 in.). Line the slices of prosciutto, slightly overlapping each other, along the bottom of the pan, letting them hang over the sides, forming a casing for the tin. Divide the meat mixture in half. Place half on the bottom and pat it down, bringing some up the sides of the tin. In the center of the tin, place the hard-boiled eggs in a row lengthwise. Top the eggs with the remaining meat mixture, pushing down to flatten and tighten the loaf. Fold the overhanging prosciutto slices over the top of the loaf and push down firmly with your hands.

Cover with foil and bake the loaf for 1 hour. Unmold it, and then continue to bake it uncovered in a baking dish until it is golden. Allow it to cool sufficiently.

In the meantime, prepare the tomato sauce. Heat the olive oil and sauté the onion until it is soft and caramelized. Add the tomato puree and sugar. Cook the mixture over medium heat for about 15 minutes. Season it with salt and pepper.

Slice the meat loaf and serve it with the tomato sauce along with fried potatoes and a Greek salad on the side.

SAUCE

¼ cup olive oil

1 onion, diced

2 cups tomato puree

2 teaspoons dark brown (muscovado) sugar

MAKES: 12 SERVINGS
TIME: 2 HOURS, 30 MINUTES

MEAT SAUCE

½ cup olive oil

3 garlic cloves, minced

250 g (8.8 oz./0.55 lb.) minced lamb*

250 g (8.8 oz./0.55 lb.) minced beef

1½ teaspoon salt

1 teaspoon black pepper

2 teaspoons cinnamon powder

½ teaspoon ground cloves

1 cinnamon quill

1 bay leaf

3 tablespoons tomato paste

2 cups tomato puree

1 cup red wine

2 cups water

2 teaspoons castor (superfine) sugar

Light olive oil, for frying

3 large eggplants, sliced into 1 cm (0.4 in.) rounds

6 large potatoes, sliced into 1 cm (0.4 in.) rounds

1 cup kefalograviera cheese†

Salt, to taste

Who has not heard of this rich and hearty dish? The subtle hint of cinnamon- and clove-spiced lamb and beef, lightly fried eggplants, and fried potatoes, all covered in a white sauce, make for an unforgettable meal. Moussaka is quite time-consuming but is positively worth the effort. Plan ahead so it won't seem too daunting on the day you plan to serve the meal. Prepare the meat sauce a day in advance. Then, early on the day of, peel the potatoes and submerge them in water until they are ready to fry. I have also provided a gluten-free option to regular white sauce, if desired. I wouldn't want anyone to miss out on moussaka!

Moussaka

Moussaka
Μουσακάς

To prepare the meat sauce, heat the oil in a medium pan over medium heat. Add the garlic and sauté until it starts to sizzle, being careful not to burn it. Add the beef and lamb to the pan. Season with salt and pepper. Using a wooden spoon, start to break up the meat, allowing it to brown well. Do not hurry this step—it is crucial to take it slowly. Brown the meats until all the juices have evaporated and the oil has come to the surface. Add the cinnamon powder, cloves, cinnamon quill, and bay leaf and cook for 1 minute. Add the tomato paste and cook for another 3 minutes. Add the tomato puree, wine, water, and sugar. Simmer the sauce over low heat, covered, until the meat is cooked, the sauce has reduced, and oil has come to the surface. This takes approximately 35–40 minutes. Set the sauce aside.

Add a few tablespoons of olive oil to a frying pan and fry the eggplants in batches until they are golden on both sides. Sprinkle them with salt and set them aside.

Fill a shallow frying pan almost to the halfway point with light olive oil. Heat over medium heat and fry the potatoes until they are golden. Set them aside, sprinkling them with salt.

Preheat the oven to 220°C (428°F).

To prepare the white sauce, place the flour in a bowl with the water. Whisk the mixture to remove any lumps (it will be a runny consistency). In a pot, add the milk and the whisked egg, mixing everything well. Add the salt.

Heat the milk well, and then add the flour batter, whisking the sauce continuously to remove any lumps, until the sauce thickens. This should take about 10 minutes (or at boiling point). Take the sauce off the stove. Add the grated nutmeg and cheese to the sauce and set it aside.

Sprinkle a tablespoon of cheese on the bottom of an ovenproof dish that measures 34 cm by 24 cm by 5 cm (13.3 in. by 9.4 in. by 2 in.). Add 1 layer of eggplant and then 1 layer of potatoes, repeating the layers and sprinkling a little cheese between each one. Pour the meat sauce on top, followed by the white sauce. Sprinkle the extra cheese, sugar, and bread crumbs on top of the white sauce. Bake the moussaka for 50 minutes or until it is golden brown. Allow it to rest for 20 minutes and then serve it with a Greek salad.

If preferred, the lamb may be omitted and the recipe made using a doubled quantity of beef.

†*Kefalograviera cheese is a hard sheep's milk cheese with a salty flavor and rich aroma. It can be found in Mediterranean delicatessens and is sold in wedges or as a wheel. Grated pecorino, Romano, or parmesan cheeses may be used as substitutes.*

‡*For a gluten-free white sauce, use 6 tablespoons corn flour (cornstarch) instead of all-purpose flour and dilute in ¼ cup water (instead of 1–2 cups water). Proceed as per the recipe.*

WHITE SAUCE

1½ cups all-purpose flour‡

1–2 cups water‡

1 L (33.8 fl. oz.) whole milk

1 egg

Salt, to taste

1 teaspoon grated fresh nutmeg

200 g (0.44 lb./7.0 oz.) grated kefalograviera cheese, plus ¼ cup extra for topping

2 teaspoons castor (superfine) sugar

2 teaspoons bread crumbs

GLUTEN-FREE
MAKES: 6 SERVINGS
PREPARATION: OVERNIGHT SOAKING
TIME: 2 HOURS, 30 MINUTES

2 cups lima beans, soaked overnight in water

½ cup olive oil

1 large onion, diced

2 garlic cloves, minced

½ teaspoon salt

2 cups tomato puree

1 teaspoon mild paprika

2 teaspoons castor (superfine) sugar

300 g (10.5 oz./0.66 lb.) butternut pumpkin, cubed into 3 cm (1.2 in.) squares

1 cup chopped celery

2 bay leaves

½ cup olive oil

½ cup white wine

1 cup water, reserved from beans

Salt, to taste

Black pepper, to taste

½ cup finely chopped flat leaf parsley

Beans are extremely popular in the Greek cuisine. From soups and stews to baked beans, they are a weekly meal eaten by the old and young alike. They are a hearty, nutritious, and a great source of fiber. Forget what you know about baked beans, or other beans in a can. Get ready to experiment with *real* beans that taste totally different and totally amazing. I have two ways you can enjoy these appetizing baked beans: a vegetarian and meat version. Pick to your heart's delight. There is something for all!

Lima Beans Two Ways

Gigantes me Lahanika
Γίγαντες με Λαχανικά

Place lima beans in a bowl of fresh cold water to soak overnight.

The next day, drain the soaked beans and add them to a pot. Fill the pot with fresh water, making sure the beans are totally submerged. Over medium heat, cook the lima beans ¾ of the way, partially covered (don't close it completely; it will froth and overflow). This should take about 40 minutes. Do not fully cook the beans, as they will cook again in the oven. Drain the pot (reserving the cooking water) and place the beans in an ovenproof dish.

Preheat the oven to 220°C (428°F).

In a sauté pan, heat the olive oil, onion, garlic, and salt, sautéing until the onion and garlic are soft but not browned. To this, add the tomato puree, paprika, and sugar. Cook the mixture for 3 minutes. Add it to a baking dish along with the pumpkin, celery, bay leaves, olive oil, wine, reserved water, salt, and pepper. Mix the ingredients well and top them with parsley.

Bake the beans, uncovered, for 1½ hours until they are tender and the sauce has reduced and thickened. Check the beans every 30 minutes in case they need more liquid (if so, add 1 cup from the reserved water at a time). Serve the beans with a drizzle of olive oil and crumbled feta cheese.

Meat Version
Γίγαντες με Χωριάτικα Λουκάνικα

Cut 3 large Greek sausages into small pieces. Fry them in a shallow pan and reserve the juices. In the meantime, assemble the dish per the vegetarian version above until just before the final stage of placing the dish in the oven. Add the sausages with all their juices to the baking dish and then bake as advised.

This recipe bears the name Lazy Housewife Cheese Pie because this pie does not have pastry crust, implying that the housewife could not be bothered to make her own pastry. Surely we all have days when we are pressed for time, have unexpected guests showing up at the door, and have to quickly contemplate what we can serve. I say, who needs pastry for every pie when this one tastes amazing without it? This is "fast food" at its best. Hold on to it for those lazy days—it's delicious and super cheesy.

Lazy Housewife Cheese Pie

Tiropita Tis Tebelas
Τυρόπιτα Της Τεμπέλας

MAKES: 8 SERVINGS
TIME: 45 MINUTES

- 1 cup whole milk
- 1 cup all-purpose flour
- 1 teaspoon baking powder
- 3 eggs, whisked together
- ½ teaspoon salt
- ½ teaspoon black pepper
- 250 g (8.8 oz./0.55 lb.) feta cheese, crumbled
- 80 g (2.8 oz.) grated yellow cheese (mozzarella or parmesan)
- 1 teaspoon dried oregano
- 1½ tablespoons sesame seeds

Preheat the oven to 190°C (374°F).

In a bowl, whisk together the milk, flour, and baking powder. Add the beaten eggs, salt, pepper, cheeses, and dried oregano. Mix the ingredients well with a wooden spoon to combine.

Pour the mixture into an oiled 20 cm (8 in.) round dish. Top it with sesame seeds and bake for 35 minutes or until it is golden. Allow the pie to cool slightly, and then slice and serve it.

GLUTEN-FREE
MAKES: 6–8 SERVINGS
TIME: 1 HOUR, 40 MINUTES

1.2 kg (approximately 6–8) baby squid, cleaned and gutted

½ cup olive oil

1 large onion, diced

2 garlic cloves, minced

¾ cup medium-grain Arborio rice

½ cup finely chopped flat leaf parsley

½ cup finely chopped mint

½ cup finely chopped dill

2 tablespoons tomato paste

1 tablespoon tomato ketchup

1 cup tomato puree

½ cup water

1½ teaspoon salt

1½ teaspoon black pepper

Zest of 1 lemon

SAUCE

½ cup olive oil

1 onion, diced

1 tablespoon tomato paste

2 cups tomato puree

½ cup water

1 bay leaf

1 strip orange rind (2 cm / 1 in.)

Salt, to taste

Black pepper, to taste

½ cup finely chopped flat leaf parsley

1 lemon, for serving

Anything stuffed with rice and herbs and huddled in tomato sauce catches my direct attention, so this squid dish is certainly one I appreciate. Admittedly, stuffing squid is a little time-consuming, but it is thoroughly worth the effort. It tastes fantastic and looks visually appealing on the plate. My father-in-law, the fisherman of the family, definitely gets the praise for anything with seafood in my book. He challenged me to gut and clean my first fish when I was around thirteen years old. Eager to learn, I gutted and cleaned the freshly caught fish, and since then, he and I have certainly become fishing buddies. I played around with his stuffed squid ideas and have created what I think is a great representation of his thoughts.

Stuffed Squid

Gemista Kalamarakia
Γεμιστά Καλαμαράκια

Preheat the oven to 220°C (428°F).

In a sauté pan, add olive oil, onion, and garlic, sautéing until they are soft and translucent. Transfer them to a big bowl. To this bowl, add the rice, parsley, mint, dill, tomato paste, ketchup, tomato puree, water, salt, pepper, and lemon zest. Mix the ingredients well.

Take the cleaned squid and stuff them with the rice mixture. To close the squid, seal them with a toothpick. Assemble all the squid closely together in a baking dish.

To make the sauce, sauté the diced onion in olive oil until it is soft. Add the tomato paste and mix for about 1 minute to combine the ingredients. Add the tomato puree, water, bay leaf, orange peel, salt, and pepper. Simmer the sauce over medium heat for 5 minutes. Taste to see if it requires more salt. Pour this sauce over the squid and bake, covered, for 25–30 minutes. Uncover the dish and bake the squid for another 35–40 minutes or until the squid is cooked through and the juices have thickened slightly.

Top the squid with a sprinkling of chopped parsley and a squeeze of lemon juice. Serve it with a Greek salad and crusty bread (or gluten-free bread) to mop up the juices.

—

Make-ahead tip: The sauce can be prepared a day in advance and then poured over the squid just before baking.

Greece is full of fresh seafood. Fish have always fed the Greeks. Ask a Greek, and he or she will tell you how to source the freshest morsel. If the fish's eye is glistening clear, if the gills are still dripping blood, and if there is a scent of the sea, you have yourself a beauty.

Whole baked snapper, with its head and tail intact, ensures an eye-catching, favorable meal. Always ask your fishmonger to clean and scale the fish.

Baked Snapper

Snapa Sto Fourno

Σνάπα Στο Φούρνο

GLUTEN-FREE
MAKES: 4 SERVINGS
TIME: 1 HOUR, 30 MINUTES

1 whole red snapper, gutted and scaled, tail and head intact

Salt, to taste

Black pepper, to taste

1 teaspoon mild paprika

½ cup finely chopped flat leaf parsley

1 lemon, sliced

4 medium potatoes, peeled and quartered

1 large onion, diced

2 garlic cloves, peeled and sliced

¼ cup olive oil

1 tablespoon tomato paste

2 cups crushed tomatoes

½ cup white wine

1 tablespoon dried oregano

¾ cup olive oil

Preheat the oven to 220°C (428°F).

Place the cleaned snapper on a large baking dish. Score 3 incisions with a sharp knife on the top and bottom of the fish. Drizzle a little olive oil and sprinkle the salt, pepper, paprika, and pepper on both sides of the fish. Take the parsley and place it in the incisions. Place the lemon slices into the cavity of the fish. Place the potatoes around the fish. Season the fish with more salt and pepper and set it aside.

In a pan, sauté the onion and garlic with the olive oil until the onion and garlic are soft and fragrant. Add the tomato paste, crushed tomatoes, wine, and oregano. Season the sauce and simmer it for 10 minutes. Pour the sauce over the fish, adding 1 cup of cold water and the ¾ cup olive oil, and bake it for 1 hour or until the fish is cooked through. If it starts to dry out, add 1 cup of boiled water. Baste the fish occasionally with the pan juices. Serve with crusty bread (or gluten-free bread) on the side.

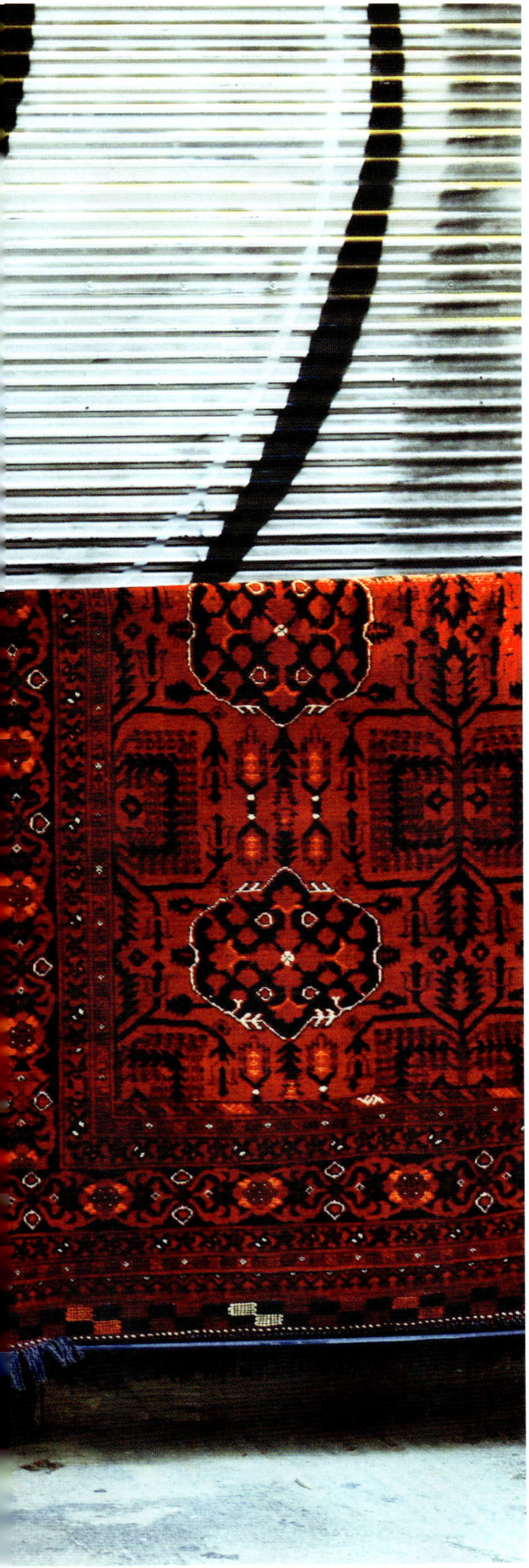

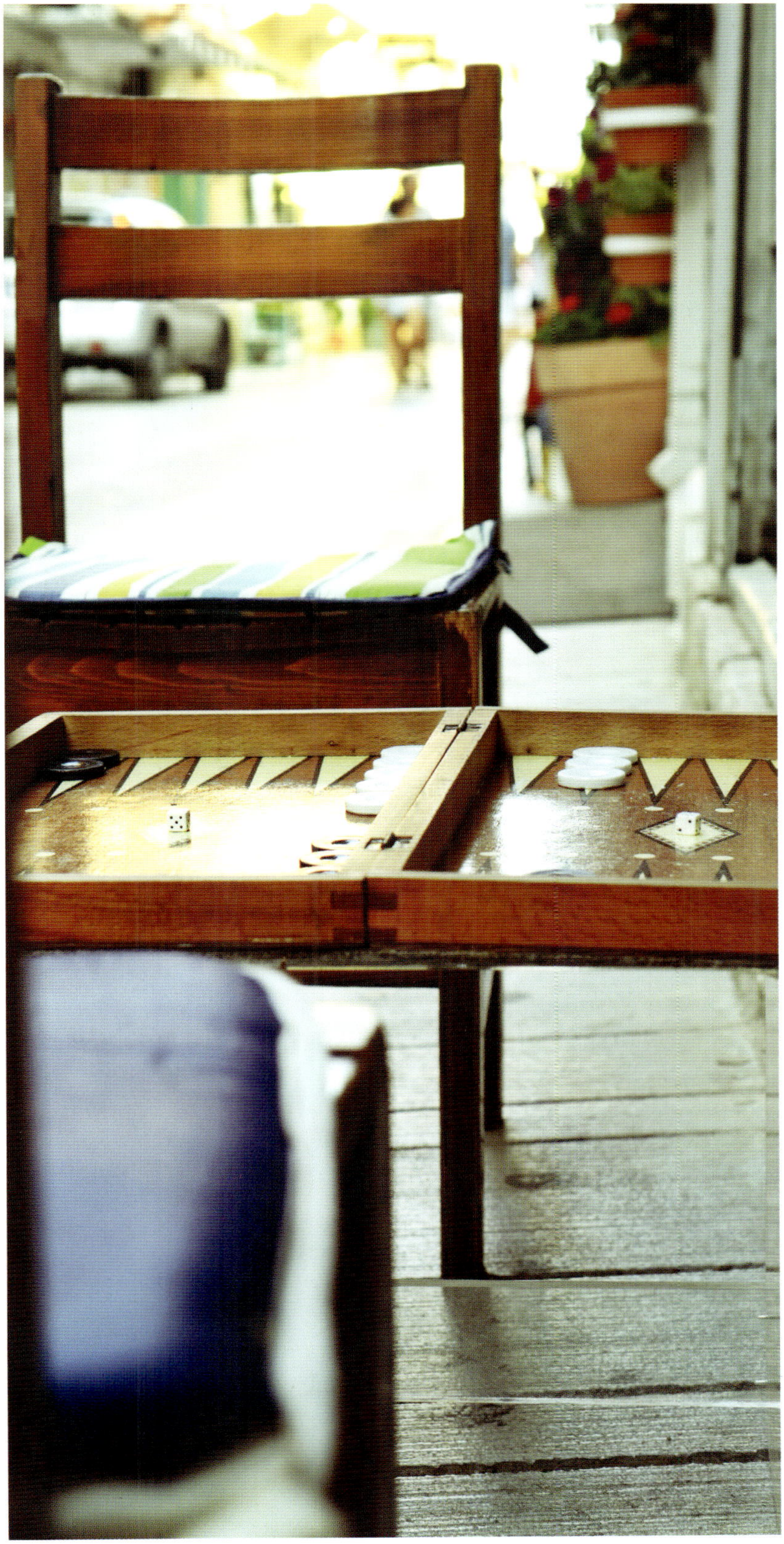

FOUR
Sweet Endings

Telionontas Glika
Τελειώνοντας Γλυκά

Milk Pie

Olive Oil Cake with Orange Blossom Syrup

Sesame, Salted Pistachio, and Rose Water Baklava

Sesame and Nut Bars (GF)

Orange-Apricot Semolina Pudding

Sweet Easter Bread

Scrunched-Up Lemon Yogurt Pie

Greek Biscotti with Orange and Honey

Ouzo Cookies with Jam

Mastiha Pudding

Prune-Stuffed, Honey-Soaked Biscuits

Orange-Scented Rice Pudding (GF)

Almond and Orange Shortbreads

Honey Donuts

Greek Yogurt Cheesecake with Ouzo Poached Figs

Sweet Pumpkin Pie

Yogurt-Olive Oil Sponge Cake

Olive Oil Pastries Stuffed with Turkish Delight

Grape Spoon Sweet (GF)

Greek Coffee

GF denotes gluten-free recipes

Sweet Endings

A Greek confectionary shop or bakery is called a *zaharoplasteio*, meaning "sugar" and "sculptor." A *zaharoplastis* is someone who molds and invents things with sugar. These shops are everywhere in Greece. The aroma is noticeable from a far distance, and it's one that cannot be resisted. The bakeries are filled with various pastries huddled with cheeses or drenched in syrup, with cream-filled biscuits, and with traditional festive treats. Greeks will purchase sweets from these bakeries and will have them delicately boxed and wrapped. Whenever a Greek visits a friend's home, especially for the first time or for a celebration, a box of these treats is always given to the host. A Greek will say, "Den tha pao me adeia heria" or "I cannot go with empty hands." A box of Greek sweets is a gesture of thankfulness.

When one thinks of dessert, automatically the thought of fatty, sweet, and unhealthy confections comes to mind. Well, this is not exactly the case for Greek sweets. Many Greek desserts are nutritious and are eaten for breakfast and snacks as well as for dessert. Help yourself to a sesame bar loaded with nuts and honey; a bowlful of rice pudding, drizzled with honey or covered in fruit; a biscotti with a cup of Greek coffee; or even a cupful of Greek yogurt with cinnamon and nuts. Feeling unhealthy or guilty while enjoying an array of great choices in the Greek sweet aisle? Sure, there are very sweet desserts, if you care for them. They are delicious and intense—you only need a small amount to satisfy that sweet craving—but there is also the wonderful alternative of healthy yet amazingly tasty desserts. The use of olive oil, honey, and spices make many Greek desserts guilt-free and actually healthy to consume. Olive oil retains moisture in the baking, and therefore sweets stay moist and last longer.

This is unquestionably a dessert you cannot resist! Every Greek cook has a take on this classic milk pie, and this is mine. It reminds me of my father. I picture him as a small child, just as he is in this photograph (page 194), waiting to be rewarded with his desired treat. He loves this dessert and always wants a slice of the pie hot from the oven. It's a special moment to watch him prepare himself with a dessert fork and knife as he waits impatiently by the oven. He cuts into the crispy, buttered layers of filo and then into the soft lemon-orange vanilla custard and takes his first bite. I wait for what I know will soon come: "Oh, this is great, Ruthy. Not too sweet—just perfect!"

I know my father deserves more than the first and best piece of this dessert, but the look in his eyes and the enjoyment he receives from this gesture—his favorite dessert done well—is priceless. It has a blend of semolina, rice flour, and corn flour that makes for a perfect, silky custard with the addition of orange blossom water. It is then soaked in a citrus syrup. This pie is best served the same day it's baked, at room temperature. With all Greek syrup cakes, you must ensure that the cake is hot and the syrup cold, or vice versa.

Milk Pie

Galaktoboureko
Γαλακτομπούρεκο

MAKES: 24 PIECES
TIME: 1 HOUR, 50 MINUTES

200 g (7.0 oz.) unsalted butter, melted

2 L (67 fl. oz.) whole milk

1 teaspoon vanilla powder or ½ vanilla bean, deseeded

1 cup castor (superfine) sugar

¾ cup semolina flour

¼ cup corn flour (cornstarch)

½ cup rice flour

3 eggs whisked together

Zest of ½ a lemon

Zest of 1 orange

250 g (16 sheets) filo pastry

Preheat the oven to 190°C (374°F).

Melt the butter in a saucepan and set it aside.

Place all the syrup ingredients (except the orange blossom water) into a pot and slowly bring them to a boil. Lower the heat and allow the mixture to simmer for 9 minutes. Pour the syrup into a bowl and allow it to cool completely in the fridge. Once it is cooled, add the orange blossom water and return the syrup to the refrigerator until the cake is cooked.

In a large saucepan, heat the milk with vanilla until it is hot but not boiling. Slowly pour in the sugar, semolina flour, corn flour, and rice flour, whisking constantly until it thickens into custard. (It will thicken at the boiling point.) Take the custard off the stove and add the beaten eggs, whisking very fast so the eggs don't scramble. Add the lemon and orange zests.

Butter a baking dish (34 cm by 24 cm/13.3 in. by 9.4 in.). Remove the filo from the packet and place the baking dish on top of it. With a sharp knife, cut 10 sheets of filo so that they fit perfectly in the dish. Set these aside and cover them with a damp cloth.

Layer 4 sheets of filo (buttering each layer) so that they extend half in the pan and half out of the pan vertically and horizontally, adding 2 more in the middle. (This creates a casing for the cream). Pour the custard into the dish. Fold the filo that is hanging out of the tray onto the custard. Layer the 10 cut filo sheets on top, ensuring they are buttered well, including the top layer. With a sharp knife, score only the top layers of filo pastry into 24 equal diamond shapes—or whatever shape you desire.

Bake the pie for 50 minutes or until the pastry has puffed up and is golden.

As soon as you remove the pie from the oven, immediately pour the cold syrup on top.

Allow the pie to cool to room temperature and then serve it. It can also be served cold the next day, directly from the fridge (although the custard hardens slightly).

—

Glucose syrup can be replaced with honey, although the taste will be slightly stronger (use 4 tablespoons of runny honey).

†Orange blossom water is sold at all international delicatessens.

SYRUP

2½ cups castor (superfine) sugar

2 cups water

1 strip lemon rind, 5 cm (2 in.) long

2 tablespoons glucose syrup*

2 tablespoons orange blossom water†

1 cinnamon quill

Milk Pie
(page 192)

I love olive oil in desserts. It is a low-fat alternative to butter and is an unsaturated fat. This cake is best eaten a day or two after baking. The flavors infuse and intensify as the cake soaks up the syrup. It is moist due to the olive oil; it is light from the semolina flour; it is tangy from the citrus; and the flavor is heightened by the orange blossom water. This cake is best accompanied with a cup of Greek coffee. It can be stored in an airtight container in the refrigerator for up to a week.

Olive Oil Cake with Orange Blossom Syrup

Revani

Ρεβανί

MAKES: 20 PIECES
TIME: 1 HOUR

1 cup light olive oil

5 eggs

½ cup castor (superfine) sugar

¾ cup freshly squeezed orange juice

Zest of 2 oranges

1 cup semolina flour

1 cup all-purpose flour

3 teaspoons baking powder

2 teaspoons cinnamon powder

1 vanilla bean, deseeded

½ teaspoon mastiha, ground*

½ cup roasted and crushed almonds

Preheat the oven to 190°C (374°F).

Place all the syrup ingredients (except the orange blossom water) in a pot. Simmer the mixture over low heat for 9 minutes. Pour the syrup into a bowl and place it in the fridge to cool. Once the syrup is cold, add the orange blossom water. Set aside.

In a mixer, beat the olive oil with the eggs for 30 seconds. Add the sugar, orange juice, orange zest, semolina flour, all-purpose flour, and baking powder. Mix the ingredients until they are well combined. At this point, the mixture may look like it is curdling, but don't worry—it will be fine. Add the cinnamon, vanilla, mastiha, and crushed almonds. Mix the ingredients again, just enough to combine.

Pour the batter into an oiled cake tin that measures 23 cm by 23 cm (9 in. by 9 in.). Bake the cake for 30 minutes. Remove the cake from the oven and carefully score it into small pieces while it is still half-cooked. Place it back into the oven for another 20 minutes or until a skewer inserted comes out clean.

Remove the cake from the oven and immediately pour the cold syrup on the cake, ensuring it all gets soaked. It will seem as though it has a lot of syrup, but don't worry—the cake will soak in all the juices and will stay moist.

Let the cake stand for 3–4 hours (or preferably for an entire day) before serving it.

—

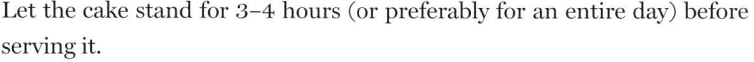

*If you do not have mastiha, you could substitute an orange liquor or ouzo.

†Glucose syrup can be replaced with honey, although the taste will be slightly stronger (use 4 tablespoons of runny honey).

‡Orange blossom water is sold at international delicatessens.

SUGAR SYRUP

2 cups castor (superfine) sugar

3 cups water

1 strip lemon rind (5 cm / 2 in.) long

2 tablespoons glucose syrup†

1 cinnamon quill

4 whole cloves

1 teaspoon orange blossom water‡

Okay, let's not get into the debate as to where this dessert originated. It is a major component of Greek cuisine today, and it captures the essence of Greek aromas in one luscious bite. Baklava is made of layers of buttered filo pastry alternating with sweetened nuts that have been drenched in sugar syrup. This recipe leaves a subtle scent of rose water lingering on the palate and has an extra nutty flavor derived from the sesame seeds. Substituting light olive oil in place of the butter also works well, making it a perfect dessert for those who steer away from dairy.

Sesame, Salted Pistachio, and Rose Water Baklava

Baklava
Μπακλαβάς

MAKES: 24 PIECES
TIME: 1 HOUR, 40 MINUTES

250 g (8.8 oz.) unsalted butter, melted

1 cup crushed almonds

1 cup crushed walnuts

¼ cup crushed salted pistachios

¼ cup toasted sesame seeds

2 teaspoons cloves

2 teaspoons cinnamon

1 teaspoon ground nutmeg

½ cup castor (superfine) sugar

450 g (14¼ oz.) filo pastry

Preheat the oven to 180°C (364°F).

Melt the butter in a saucepan and set it aside.

Place all the syrup ingredients in a pot (except the rose water) and slowly bring them to a boil. Lower the heat and simmer for 9 minutes. Pour the syrup into a bowl and allow it to cool in the fridge. Once the syrup is cold, add the rose water and place it back into the fridge to remain cold.

In a bowl, mix together the crushed nuts, cinnamon, cloves, nutmeg, sesame seeds, and sugar.

Butter a baking dish (34 cm by 24 cm/13.3 in. by 9.4 in.). Unroll the filo pastry from the package and place the baking dish on top. Cut the filo around the baking dish so that the filo will fit perfectly in the dish. Set aside 10 sheets of the filo pastry, covering them with a damp cloth until they are needed.

Using the remaining filo pastry, take 5 sheets and line the baking dish, drizzling some butter on each layer. Sprinkle 2 heaping tablespoons of the nut mixture onto the filo. Cover this layer with 2 more sheets of buttered pastry and sprinkle 2½ tablespoons of the nut mixture over this layer. Repeat this process until all the nut mixture is used.

Top the baklava with the 10 sheets of pastry reserved in the beginning, ensuring that each layer is well buttered, including the top layer.

Place the baklava in the fridge for 10 minutes—this makes the scoring easier. Then, with a sharp knife, cut through the top layers of filo pastry, forming portion sizes of your choice.

Bake the baklava for 35–40 minutes or until the pastry has puffed up and is a golden color.

As soon as the baklava has been removed from the oven, immediately pour the cold syrup on top. Allow it to cool completely and then serve it. Baklava can be stored in the fridge for up to a week.

Best served with Greek coffee and a glass of iced water!

—

Suggestion: Do not increase the cooking temperature; this will cause the baklava to cook on the top, but the inside layers will remain raw.

*Glucose syrup can be replaced with honey, although the taste will be slightly stronger (use 4 tablespoons of runny honey).

†Rose water is sold at international delicatessens.

SUGAR SYRUP

2½ cups castor (superfine) sugar

2 cups water

1 strip lemon rind (5 cm / 2 in.) long

2 tablespoons glucose syrup*

1 cinnamon quill

3 tablespoons rose water†

Sesame, Salted Pistachio, and Rose Water Baklava (page 198)

As a child in Greek school, I would sit at my wooden desk looking at the blackboard and thinking about the crunchy little sesame bar in my lunch box. This was a Greek child's candy bar! The smell of the nuts and honey, as well as the little bits of sesame getting caught between my teeth, was so much fun for me as a child. This is the energy bar of Greek sweets, documented and dated back to ancient Greece. It is a chewy, nutty bar that seems bad for you but is actually a nutritious vegan treat. Whether you eat this as a snack, a breakfast bar, or a dessert with a cup of coffee, this will without a doubt give you a boost to keep you going. I have added some mastiha, chopped nougat, and nuts to make it that much more delectable.

Sesame and Nut Bars

Pasteli
Παστέλι

GLUTEN-FREE
MAKES: 25 PIECES
TIME: 35 MINUTES

3 cups sesame seeds

½ cup honey

1 cup brown (muscovado) sugar

2 teaspoons cinnamon powder

1 teaspoon lemon juice

2 tablespoons mastiha liquor or 1 teaspoon mastiha powder*

¼ cup roasted, unsalted pistachios, chopped

½ cup chopped nougat (optional)

In a sauté pan, brown the sesame seeds over low heat, being careful not to burn them. Place them in a bowl and set them aside.

Sprinkle a shallow baking tray (22 cm by 30 cm/9 in. by 11 in.) with a little water and then line it with cling film (the water helps the cling film stick). Set the tray aside.

In a saucepan, combine the honey, sugar, cinnamon, and lemon juice and bring the ingredients to a boil. Turn off the stove and immediately add the mastiha, toasted sesame, pistachios, and nougat, mixing them together quickly. The mixture may start to solidify, so you must work quickly.

Pour the mixture onto your prepared tray and then place some parchment paper on top, pressing down with your hands to flatten the sesame mixture. The thickness should be around 1½ cm (0.6 in.). Place the tray in your refrigerator for 15 minutes.

Turn the sesame mixture out on a chopping board, remove the cling film, and cut the mixture into bars with a sharp, wet knife. Store the bars in a container for up to 1 month. Place parchment paper between each layer so they don't stick together.

—

If you do not have mastiha, you could substitute an orange liquor or ouzo. Alternatively, you can omit all alcohol.

My mother-in-law always remembers this recipe using this method: "One, two, three, and four!" She would say "one" for oil, "two" for semolina, "three" for sugar, and "four" for water. I have opted to lessen the sugar and additionally include dried fruits and citrus zest. This cake really resembles something closer to a pudding than a cake. Its texture is fascinating. The semolina flour, which is toasted in olive oil, feels like tiny balls in the mouth and has a punch of spice, nuts, citrus, and fruit. This pudding is made on the stove and then unmolded to expose an array of nuts and the scent of cinnamon. It consists of humble ingredients that transform into an exquisite dessert. Once again, it shows the complexity and versatility that olive oil brings to Greek desserts. This dessert is best served cold or at room temperature.

Orange-Apricot Semolina Pudding

Halvas me Portokali
Χαλβάς με Πορτοκάλι

MAKES: 25 PIECES
TIME: 45 MINUTES

1 cup light olive oil

2 cups coarse semolina flour

3 tablespoons sesame seeds

1 teaspoon cinnamon powder

¼ cup slivered almonds

½ teaspoon vanilla powder

¼ cup sultanas or raisins

½ cup dried apricots, chopped

Zest of ½ an orange

½ cup desiccated coconut

SUGAR SYRUP

1¼ cups castor (superfine) sugar

4 cups water

1 tablespoon orange blossom water*

Rind of ½ an orange

To prepare the syrup, place all the ingredients in a pot and bring them to a boil. Simmer the syrup over very low heat while you work on the rest of the dessert.

In another pot, brown the semolina flour with the olive oil and sesame seeds over medium heat until the semolina begins to change to a golden-brown color and it starts to smell a little. Do not rush this step—it should take approximately 10–15 minutes. The semolina must be browned; otherwise, the taste of the completed dessert will be doughy.

When the flour is golden brown, add all of the remaining ingredients. Mix the ingredients well to combine, and then immediately take the mixture off the heat.

Discard the orange rind from the sugar syrup and pour the syrup into the semolina, standing back as it will bubble and splash a little (be very careful not to burn yourself). Start stirring the mixture vigorously until it comes away from the sides of the pot and has thickened into a pudding-like consistency.

Pour the pudding into a 25 cm (9.8 in.) diameter nonstick mold, pressing down with a spoon so that it is distributed evenly. Allow the pudding to cool before unmolding it onto a serving plate. Dust it with a sprinkling of cinnamon powder. This dessert is best served cold.

—

*Orange blossom water is sold at all international delicatessens.

This bread is light yet luxurious with the aromatic spice of mahlepi (see pantry item on page 37). This bread can be dunked into a glass of milk, toasted with jam, or even eaten with a slice of cheese. This traditional Easter bread is served in Greece to break the Lenten fast. It is traditionally braided with red-dyed eggs inserted as a decoration. Every Greek knows that the red eggs symbolize Jesus Christ's blood. I am thankful that the Bible clearly articulates that traditions are not what pay the penalty for our sin. Rather, our debt was paid by the shedding of Jesus's blood on the cross of Calvary so "that whosoever believes in Him shall not perish but have eternal life" (John 3:15).

Sweet Easter Bread

Tsoureki
Τσουρέκι

MAKES: 4 LARGE LOAVES

TIME: 6 HOURS, 30 MINUTES «INCLUDES RISING AND BAKING TIMES»

red food coloring, specific for dyeing eggs (sold at most supermarkets)

8 hard-boiled eggs

75 g (2.64 oz./0.16 lb.) instant yeast

2 cups warm water

3 tablespoons all-purpose flour

315 g (11 oz.) unsalted butter

1 cup whole milk

500 g (17.6 oz.) castor (superfine) sugar

8 eggs

2 teaspoons mastiha, crushed*

Dye the hard-boiled eggs as directed on the package of food dye. Set them aside to cool.

Dissolve the yeast in 2 cups of warm water, mixing in 3 tablespoons of flour. Put the mixture in a warm place to double in size.

In a saucepan, melt the butter with the milk. Remove the mixture from the heat, add the sugar, eggs, mahlepi, mastiha, and orange zest and whisk everything well to combine.

Add this mixture to a large bowl and slowly add the yeast mixture (which has doubled in size) and the flour little by little, mixing the ingredients well (or, if you are using a stand mixer, combine the ingredients in the mixer with a dough hook). Add extra flour if the mixture is too wet.

Mix the dough on medium-high speed until the dough comes away from the sides of the bowl. Alternately, you can remove the dough from the bowl, place onto the kitchen counter, and knead it by hand for approximately 10 minutes. The dough should be neither stiff nor sticky. If your hands are sticking to it, oil them, and continue to knead until your dough is soft and pliable.

Divide the dough in half and place the halves into 2 big bowls. Cover the bowls with tea towels and allow the dough to rise for 3 hours.

Once the dough has risen, divide each half in half again (you should have 4 portions in total). Take each piece and divide it into 3 equal portions. Gently roll each portion into a long rope. Plait the ropes, tucking the top and bottom ends neatly underneath and adding 1 or 2 dyed eggs into the plaiting. Repeat this process with the other dough pieces. Place the loaves on a lined baking tray. Brush the loaves with mastiha liquor and sprinkle the slivered almonds on top. Place the plaited breads, covered with a clean tea towel, in a warm place and allow them to rise a second time, around 2 hours.

Preheat the oven to 190°C (374°F) and bake the bread for about 45 minutes or until the loaves are golden in color.

—

Suggestion: You could also make a bread roll shape and fill the inside with some chocolate pieces or plait the dough and use a circular tin to make a wreath shape.

*Mastiha is available at international delicatessens.

†Mahlepi is also available at international delicatessens. Alternatively, you may use ouzo liquor.

4 tablespoons mahlepi†

Zest of 2 oranges

1 kg (35 oz. / 2.2 lb.) all-purpose flour

¾ cup slivered almonds

¼ cup mastiha liquor

Sweet Easter Bread (page 206)

Scrunched-Up Lemon Yogurt Pie

Patsavouropita
Πατσαβουρόπιτα

This is a mellow, refreshing, light ending to any meal. It has a subtle tang from the lemon and a coolness from the Greek yogurt. It boasts a custard-like filling made with olive oil and yogurt. This pie can be eaten cold or hot. It is a simple yet delicious dessert.

Dust the pie liberally with icing sugar just before serving. Refrigerate it for a few hours prior to plating, as the flavors infuse and continue to intensify. This recipe is a very refreshing dessert that is quick and easy.

SERVES: 10 PEOPLE
TIME: 1 HOUR

1 cup Greek yogurt

1 cup light olive oil

½ cup castor (superfine) sugar

1 cup whole milk

3 eggs

1 teaspoon vanilla powder or 1 vanilla bean, deseeded

½ teaspoon baking powder

Zest of 2 lemons

250 g (8 oz./0.55 lb.) filo pastry

Icing (confectioner's) sugar, to dust

SUGAR SYRUP

1 cup castor (superfine) sugar

2 cups water

1 teaspoon lemon juice

Preheat the oven to 190°C (374°F). Oil a 29 cm (11in.) round ovenproof dish.

In a saucepan, combine the syrup ingredients. Bring them to a boil and simmer them for 6 minutes. Set the syrup aside to cool.

In a bowl, add the yogurt, oil, sugar, milk, eggs, vanilla, baking powder, and lemon zest and mix the ingredients with a whisk to combine. Set this mixture aside.

Take 1 sheet of filo pastry and gather it into pleats. Place it into your round dish, creating a coil shape from the center. Repeat this process with the remaining filo sheets until the dish is full. Pour the yogurt mixture slowly onto the filo, starting from the middle coil and moving outward in a circular motion until the filo is all covered. Separate the layers slightly with a spoon so that the mixture seeps into all the layers.

Bake the pie for 45 minutes or until the pastry is golden and puffed.

Immediately pour the cold syrup onto the hot pie. Allow the pie to sit for 4 hours or overnight in the fridge before serving.

These biscuits, with their freshly squeezed orange juice, nuts, and olive oil, showcase my mother's intentions of making us children understand the beauty of a healthy snack. I love the fact that everything she made had as much nutrition as possible. A jar of these biscuits stands conveniently on my kitchen counter at all times. Every time I see them disappear, I make another batch. I've always loved the combination of olive oil, cinnamon, oranges, and honey, and these have all that in one bite. They are twice baked using the method of biscotti, giving them that great crunch. The crunchier the biscuit, the better the effect of that Greek-coffee dunk—it slightly softens the biscuit, but the biscuit still retains its slightly crumbly texture.

Entice your guests with these inviting, tasty little treats. They are a great, guilt-free biscuit.

Greek Biscotti with Orange and Honey

Paximadia Me Portokali Kai Meli
Παξιμάδια Με Πορτοκάλι Και Μέλι

MAKES: 50 BISCUITS
TIME: 1 HOUR

3 eggs

1 cup olive oil

½ cup freshly squeezed orange juice

Zest of 1 orange

¾ cup runny honey

½ cup ouzo liquor*

1½ cups castor (superfine) sugar

1 teaspoon baking powder

2½ teaspoons cinnamon powder

2½ teaspoons cloves

1½ cups raw almonds, chopped

1½ kg (35.2 oz. /3.3 lb.) all-purpose flour

¼ cup sesame seeds

Preheat the oven to 190°C (374°F).

In a stand mixer with the paddle attachment in place, add the eggs, olive oil, orange juice, orange zest, honey, and liquor and mix the ingredients well to combine. To this mixture add the sugar, baking powder, cinnamon, cloves, and nuts. With the mixer on low, slowly incorporate the flour, adding a cup at a time until the ingredients are combined.

Transfer the dough to a floured surface and roll it into a long log (add flour if it is too sticky). Divide the dough into 4 logs measuring 20 cm by 6 cm (7.8 in. by 2.3 in.). Sprinkle sesame seeds onto the bench and roll the logs in them.

Line 2 baking trays and place 2 logs on each tray. Bake the logs for 25 minutes or until they are a little firm. Remove them from the oven and cut diagonal slices measuring 1½ cm (0.6 in.) with a serrated knife. Put the slices back on the tray in a single layer and bake them for another 15 minutes. Turn the oven off and allow the biscuits to cool in the oven.

Store these biscuits in an airtight container for up to 3 weeks.

—

*Ouzo liquor can be substituted with orange liquor.

Whenever I see these sandwiched cookies, my mother-in-law comes to mind. Years before my husband and I got married, she had made a substantial batch (very traditional by her standards) and gifted them to my mother. At the time, I was intrigued at how professional they looked and was dismayed that they were actually homemade. My desire to stretch my cooking skills and attempt to make them was immediate. I set a date with her, and she graciously offered to come to my home and teach me. Nearly twenty years later, I still make them exactly as she taught me.

This batter is made with butter, and while I'm not the biggest fan of using butter, I chose to stay true to my mother-in-law's recipe. Buttery ouzo cookies sandwiched with marmalade and dunked into nuts and chocolate are a common cookie variety in Greek bakeries.

Ouzo Cookies with Jam

Biskota Me Ouzo Kai Marmelada
Μπισκότα Με Ούζο Και Μαρμελάδα

MAKES: 50 BISCUITS «100 HALVES»
TIME: 2 HOURS «WITH COOLING TIME»

250 g (8.8 oz. /0.55 lb.) unsalted butter, at room temperature

3 eggs, at room temperature

1 tsp vanilla extract

⅓ cup ouzo liquor*

1 cup castor (superfine) sugar

900 g (31.7 oz./1.9 lb.) self-rising flour

125 g (4.4 oz./0.27 lb.) marmalade†

125 g (4.4 oz./0.27 lb.) dark chocolate (at least 70% cocoa)

125 g (4.4 oz./0.27 lb.) white chocolate

½ cup crushed peanuts

Preheat the oven to 190°C (374°F).

Beat the room-temperature butter in a mixer on medium speed for 10–15 minutes or until it is fluffy and white in color. Gradually add the eggs, combining the ingredients well. (At this stage, it may look as though it has curdled, but don't worry—once the flour is added, it will be fine.)

Add the vanilla, ouzo, and sugar, and then gradually add half of the flour. Mix the ingredients to combine, and then pour the mixture onto a clean bench, adding the remaining flour. Knead this mixture with your hands until you have dough that does not stick. Allow the dough to rest, covered with a tea towel, for 15 minutes.

Using a cookie press, make your desired shape. Remember that 2 biscuits will be sandwiched together, so make sure you make an even number. Place the cookies on a baking tray.

Bake the cookies for 15 minutes. Check on them every 5 minutes, because you do not want them overdone or dark. Allow the cookies to cool.

Spread some marmalade on 1 cookie, and then top this with another cookie to form a completed cookie.

Chop the white and dark chocolate into small pieces and place them into 2 separate heatproof bowls. Fill two saucepans with water, bring both to a boil, and then reduce them to a simmer. Place the bowls with the chocolate on top of the saucepans and allow the chocolate to slowly melt. Once they have melted, dip 1 side of the cookie into the chocolate (white or dark). Then, dip the chocolate side into the nuts. Allow the cookies to dry on a baking sheet. Store them in an airtight container in the fridge for up to 2 weeks.

—

*Ouzo liquor can be substituted with amaretto liquor.

†My preference is a mixture of orange and raspberry marmalade.

Ouzo Cookies with Jam
(page 214)

Mastiha Pudding
(page 218)

This dessert reformed my entire perception of creamy cakes. I was by no means one to delight in creamy things in general until my husband insisted I try *Ekmek*. Well, where do I begin? It's astoundingly refreshing. The lightness of the custard in contrast to the syrupy pastry with the unique flavor delicately balanced by the surprisingly unpredicted mastiha is incredible. I think I have been won over by this amazing compilation. It resembles a trifle and is best made a day in advance. The origin of this dessert is from Turkey, but Greeks have adapted it with the use of mastiha, which is grown only in Greece. It is delicious served with a sour cherry spoon sweet purchased from international delicatessens.

Mastiha Pudding

Ek Mek me Mastiha
Εκμέκ με Μαστίχα

MAKES: 20 PIECES
TIME: 4 HOURS, OR BEST CHILLED OVERNIGHT

250 g (8.8 oz./0.55 lb.) kataifi pastry*

1 tablespoon cinnamon powder, divided

1 L (33.8 fl. oz.) whole milk

1 teaspoon vanilla sugar

6 eggs

1 cup castor (superfine) sugar

100 g (3.5 oz. /0.22 lb.) all-purpose flour

1 teaspoon mastiha powder†

6 tablespoons mastiha liquor,‡ divided

500 mL (16.9 fl. oz.) thickened cream (heavy cream)

Place the syrup ingredients in a pot and bring them to a boil. Simmer the syrup over medium heat for 6 minutes. Place the syrup in a bowl and allow it to cool completely in the fridge.

Preheat the oven to 190°C (374°F).

On a bench, pull apart the kataifi with your fingers until all the strands are loose and not clumped together.

PASTRY TOPPING:

Separate 100 g (3.5 oz./0.22 lb.) of pastry and spread it in a baking dish and sprinkle with ½ tablespoon of the cinnamon powder

Bake the pastry at 190°C (374°F) for 10 minutes or until it is golden. Set the pastry aside.

BOTTOM LAYER:

Take the remaining 150 g (5.2 oz. /0.33 lb.) of kataifi and layer this on the bottom of a baking dish that measures 34 cm by 24 cm by 6 cm (13 in. by 9 in. by 2.3 in.). Sprinkle the remaining ½ tablespoon of cinnamon powder on top and bake it for 20 minutes or until it is golden brown. Remove the pastry from the oven and immediately pour the sugar syrup on top. Allow the pastry to stand until all the syrup has been soaked into the kataifi. Set it aside and allow it to cool.

MIDDLE LAYER:

In a saucepan, heat the milk and vanilla (but do not boil them). In a separate bowl, mix the eggs, sugar, and flour, whisking the ingredients to combine. Pour the warm milk into the egg mixture, stirring well, and immediately pour the mixture back into the saucepan. Keep stirring the mixture with a whisk over low heat until you have thickened custard (approximately 10–15 minutes or until it starts to boil). Add the crushed mastiha and mastiha liquor. Mix all the ingredients to combine. Pour into a bowl, place some cling film directly onto the custard, and allow it to cool completely. This will prevent a skin from forming on the custard. Once it has cooled, remove the cling film and pour the custard on top of the kataifi layer, spreading it around evenly.

TOP LAYER:

Whip the thickened cream with the 3 tablespoons of liquor until soft peaks form. Pour this on top of the custard layer.

Place the pudding in the fridge for at least 2 hours. Sprinkle the baked kataifi topping on top of the dessert. Lightly sprinkle on a little more cinnamon powder. Keep the pudding refrigerated until you're ready to eat.

Kataifi pastry is available at all international delicatessens.

†*Mastiha powder is available at all international delicatessens.*

‡*As an alternative, you can replace mastiha liquor with ouzo or an almond liquor.*

SUGAR SYRUP

2 cups castor (superfine) sugar

2½ cups water

1 cinnamon quill

MAKES: 35 PIECES
TIME: 1 HOUR, 40 MINUTES

PRUNE STUFFING

300 grams (10.5 oz.) pitted prunes

½ cup freshly squeezed orange juice

Zest of 1 orange

BISCUIT INGREDIENTS

2 eggs

1½ cups olive oil

1½ cups castor (superfine) sugar

2 teaspoons ground cinnamon

1 teaspoon ground clove

Zest of 1 lemon

Zest of 1 orange

1 teaspoon baking soda

1 cup freshly squeezed orange juice

1½ kg (52.9 oz. /3.3 lb.) self-rising flour

2–3 cups crushed walnuts

SUGAR SYRUP

2 cups honey

½ cup castor (superfine) sugar

1 cup water

½ an orange

8 cloves

Melted honey and baked cinnamon are two aromas that communicate Christmas to one's senses, and the aroma of these biscuits is no exception. These biscuits are drenched in honey syrup and spiced with cinnamon and orange to create a melt-in-the-mouth biscuit. They are made religiously during Christmas and New Year's. They remain moist because of the olive oil, and they improve in flavor, making them great biscuits to have in the kitchen for at least one month in a sealed container. This recipe has been a family favorite from my Auntie Margaret. I have adapted the recipe with a prune stuffing.

Prune-Stuffed, Honey-Soaked Biscuits

Gemista Melomakarona me Damaskina
Γεμιστά Μελομακάρονα με Δαμάσκηνα

Preheat the oven to 190°C (374°F).

Place the stuffing ingredients in a saucepan. Cover them with water and allow them to simmer until half the liquid has evaporated. Take the stuffing ingredients off the heat and mash them with a potato masher to create a paste. Set the paste aside to cool.

Place the eggs, olive oil, sugar, cinnamon, cloves, lemon zest, and orange zest into the bowl of a stand mixer. Mix the ingredients until they are combined. In a bowl, combine the baking soda with the orange juice (it will fizz) and then add it to the mixer. On medium speed, mix everything until it is combined. Gradually add the flour a little at a time until a soft, pliable dough is formed that is not too hard or too sticky when rolled in your palms. Stop adding flour once this is achieved.

With your hands, take a piece of dough and roll it into an oval-shaped ball the size of a large walnut. Create a little indentation and add 1 teaspoon of the prune paste. Enclose the paste and then gently roll the dough into a ball. Flatten the dough slightly and place it on a baking tray.

Bake the biscuits for 20–30 minutes or until they are lightly golden.

Place the syrup ingredients in a saucepan and bring them to a boil. Reduce the heat to low and dunk each biscuit into the honey mixture for about 1 minute, flipping it over to ensure it is soaked evenly on both sides. Do not let the biscuits soak too long or they will fall apart. Immediately sprinkle the biscuits with walnuts and enjoy!

Just as the title states, this dessert is a rice (*rizo*) and milk (*gala*) pudding that is generously enriched with citrus rinds. It resembles thick custard; with no eggs or butter, however, it remains perfectly light, fluffy, and delicious. This dish is certainly a labor of love, as it is cooked over low heat and, for best results, stirred continuously. It can be eaten warm or straight from the fridge. It is only slightly sweetened; therefore, a further drizzling of honey or a serving of a Greek spoon sweet can be added. Always use full-cream milk for fuller flavor.

Orange-Scented Rice Pudding

Rizogalo
Ρυζόγαλο

GLUTEN-FREE
MAKES: 5 SERVINGS
TIME: 45 MINUTES

1 L (33.8 fl. oz.) whole milk

½ cup medium-grain Arborio rice

1 cinnamon quill

1 vanilla bean, deseeded

1 strip lemon peel, 5 cm (2 in.) long

¼ of 1 orange, zested

1 tablespoon corn flour (cornstarch)

2 tablespoons castor (superfine) sugar

Cinnamon powder, to dust

Place the milk, rice, cinnamon quill, vanilla, lemon rind, and orange zest into a saucepan. Over medium to low heat, allow the rice to cook until soft, whisking or stirring with a wooden spoon so it doesn't stick. The more it is stirred, the better. This should take approximately 40 minutes. When the rice is cooked, remove the lemon rind and cinnamon quill.

Dilute the corn flour with ¼ cup of water in a small bowl. Pour it into the rice mixture, whisking until it is combined and the pudding has thickened. Remove the pudding from the heat. Add the sugar and mix well with a wooden spoon.

Pour the pudding into 5 serving bowls and liberally sprinkle with cinnamon powder.

This pudding can be eaten warm or cold, drizzled with some Greek honey, or served with a Greek spoon sweet.

—

Fact: On the Island of Kephalonia, rice pudding is called rizada. Ladies on the island would invite guests to their homes, and each serving of rice pudding had the person's name dusted on it with cinnamon powder.

Twenty years later, I still have a small piece of paper my mother-in-law gave me with a list of Greek ingredients to make these shortbreads. Problem was, there was not much else. True to Greek tradition, you don't follow a recipe per se. It's all by word of mouth, touch and smell. This stimulated me even further to learn how to make them and to recreate my own version. Always served at wedding celebrations, at Christmas, and at Easter, these shortbreads accompany the buffet and are served with a glass of cold water.

So, with a hint of orange blossom water and a snowy dusting of icing sugar, these are divine. Traditionally, they are made only with butter, but I have added olive oil, which gives them a more crumbly texture. The abundance of nuts lends a lovely crunch, and the orange zest gives a beautiful freshness.

Almond and Orange Shortbreads

Kourabiethes me Portokali kai Amigdala
Κουραμπιέδες με Πορτοκάλι και Αμύγδαλα

MAKES: 50 COOKIES
TIME: 1 HOUR, 30 MINUTES

220 g (7.7 oz. /0.48 lb.) unsalted butter, at room temperature

280 ml (9.4 fl oz. /0.6 lb.) olive oil

2 eggs

2 teaspoons vanilla powder or extract

1 teaspoon baking powder

1 tablespoon orange zest

¾ cup ouzo liquor

¼ cup orange blossom water*

¾ cup icing (confectioner's) sugar

1 cup roasted and crushed almonds

¼ cup crushed pistachios

1 kg (35.2 oz. /2.2 lb.) all-purpose flour

TOPPING

½ cup orange blossom water

3 cups sifted icing (confectioner's) sugar

Preheat the oven to 190°C (374°F).

In a mixer, beat the butter with the olive oil until the mixture is white and fluffy, about 20 minutes (the more you beat it, the better). Add the eggs 1 at a time, beating continuously. Add the vanilla, baking powder, orange zest, ouzo, orange blossom water, and icing sugar. At this point, remove the whisk and use the paddle attachment. Add the almonds and pistachios to the bowl. Mix the ingredients well, and then slowly add flour by the spoonful until you have a doughlike consistency. You know the dough is ready when you can roll up a ball in your hand and it doesn't stick.

Roll out the dough on a floured work surface and, with a rolling pin or with your hands, bring the dough together and flatten it to about 1½ cm (0.6 in.). Using a cookie cutter, cut out your desired shape from the dough. (Traditionally, these biscuits are made into half-moon shapes, but you can do whatever you like.)

Place the cookies on a baking tray and bake them for about 20 minutes or until they are just starting to go golden. You do not want them to be too dark. Remove from oven and immediately brush each cookie with orange blossom water. Allow them to cool slightly (about 8 minutes), and then sprinkle the icing sugar over them. Once they have cooled completely, place them in a jar.

*Orange blossom water is sold at international delicatessens.

Tip: To serve, sprinkle a little more icing (confectioner's) sugar on top.

Honey Donuts
(page 229)

*My mother,
Australia 1970*

These are the Greeks' version of donuts! Named honey tokens, they were served as a treat to the winners at the Olympic Games. Honey at that time was the same price as gold, so this was the ideal treat for the gold medalists. This is the oldest recorded dessert in Greek history and is also known to be the first donut in the world. When I eat these donuts, it somehow reminds me of the '70s: bold colors, fancy glassware, flared pants, and funky Volkswagens. My parents are unquestionably great representatives of this style! Though I was just a toddler during this era, I find myself thinking back to my parents and recollecting memories, bizarrely tying them together with these funky, airy, honey-drenched dough balls. Whatever the case, I'm sure they are easily shared in any decade.

Honey Donuts

Loukoumades
Λουκουμάδες

MAKES: 45 DONUTS
TIME: 1 HOUR «WITH RISING TIME»

2 cups all-purpose flour

Zest of 1 orange

2 tablespoons instant yeast

¼ cup castor (superfine) sugar

310 mL (10.4 fl. oz.) warm water, plus a little more

4–6 cups light olive oil for frying (½ full saucepan)

1–2 cups light runny honey*

Cinnamon powder for sprinkling

½ cup crushed walnuts

Mix the flour, orange zest, yeast, sugar, and water together in a large bowl until you have a slightly thick but runny batter soft enough to drop from a spoon. You may need to add more water as you go until you get the required consistency. Whisk the batter to remove any lumps and set it aside to rise for 35–45 minutes.

Once the batter has risen, tap the bowl on the counter to knock out some of the air.

Heat the oil in a deep saucepan. (It does not need to be very wide—less than 20 cm (8 in.) in diameter is best.)

To check whether your oil is hot enough, drop in a small amount of dough. It should immediately sizzle and rise to the top. If this is not happening, wait; otherwise, you will get very dense donuts, and this is not what you want.

Using an ice cream scoop, drop a spoonful of batter into the hot oil. Fry the donuts until they are a very light golden color. Remove them with a slotted spoon, immediately sprinkling them with cinnamon and drizzling them with runny honey. These are best eaten hot, served with vanilla ice cream.

—

Light honey is generally lighter in color and milder in flavor.

Greece and cheesecake—who would have guessed? Yes, cheesecake is known to have originated in ancient Greece. At that time, the use of mizithra cheese was more common. To expand on this Greek phenomenon, this recipe has a unique taste from the goat's cheese and the Greek yogurt. This keeps the mixture both tangy and sweet. I have prepared a fig, orange, and ouzo compote that works wonderfully well with the cheesecake. If you are a cheesecake lover, this will definitely impress.

Greek Yogurt Cheesecake with Ouzo Poached Figs

Glikia Tiropita Me Ouzo kai Sika
Γλυκιά Τυρόπιτα Με Ούζο και Σύκα

GLUTEN-FREE*
MAKES: 16 SERVINGS
PREP: 15 MINUTES
BAKING: 1 HOUR

CRUST

250 g (8.8 oz./0.55 lb.) plain, sweet tea cookies crushed into fine bread crumbs*

7 tablespoons (100g/3.6 oz.) melted butter

½ tablespoon cinnamon powder

Pinch of salt

CHEESECAKE MIXTURE

460 g (16.2 oz./1.0 lb.) cream cheese, at room temperature

310 g (10.9 oz./0.68 lb.) goat cheese

345 g (12.1 oz./0.76 lb.) strained Greek yogurt

4 eggs

1¾ cups castor (superfine) sugar

1 vanilla bean, deseeded

Preheat the oven to 190°C (374°F).

Double wrap the outside of a 20 cm (8 inch) springform cake pan with aluminum foil. (This ensures that no water seeps into the cheesecake and that no cheese mixture leaks out while cooking in the water bath).

Place the crushed cookies, melted butter, cinnamon, and salt in a bowl. Mix the ingredients well with a fork, and then pour them into the cake pan. Press down with the back of a spoon on the bottom of the pan to cover the base evenly. Place the crust in the fridge while proceeding with the next step.

In a mixer, beat the cream cheese, goat cheese, and yogurt until they are light and fluffy. Add the remaining ingredients, adding the eggs 1 at a time and beating them in well. Mix until all the ingredients are combined smoothly.

Remove the cake pan from the fridge and pour in the filling. Place the pan on a baking tray that fits the cake pan and has some depth. Pour boiling water into the baking tray ensuring the water is halfway up the side. Bake for 1 hour or until the filling is set and the cake has a slight golden color. Turn the oven off and allow the cheesecake to cool completely in the oven. This will ensure the cake does not crack.

To make the fig topping, place all the topping ingredients in a saucepan and bring them to a boil. Simmer the mixture over low heat for 30 minutes. Remove the figs and chop them into small pieces. Add them back to the syrup and simmer them for another 10 minutes or until the sauce has thickened and is reduced by half. (Take note that it will also set as it cools.) Cool the mixture completely.

Remove the cooled cake from the oven. Place it on a platter and remove the cheesecake from the pan. Refrigerate the cheesecake for a minimum of 2 hours before serving.

Serve with the ouzo poached figs.

—

For a gluten-free version, replace the sweet tea cookies with a gluten-free variety.

†*Rose water can be purchased from international delicatessens.*

FIG TOPPING

15 large (or 25 small) dried, whole figs

2 cups water

½ cup ouzo liquor

1 cinnamon stick

Zest of 1 orange

¾ cup castor (superfine) sugar

1 teaspoon rose water†

1 star anise

Pinch of salt

Pinch of ground black pepper

Greek Yogurt Cheesecake with Ouzo Poached Figs (page 230)

Pumpkin is a great vegetable that is sweet on its own but that becomes even more delicious when combined with spices, nuts, and sultanas. These types of sweet vegetable pies remind me of my childhood. Mum would mischievously add pumpkin to pies (a very Peloponnese ingredient), so this is an adaptation of her recipe. It is dairy- and egg-free and very delicious. It's great for breakfast with a cup of Greek coffee or served with vanilla ice cream.

Sweet Pumpkin Pie

Glikia Kolokithopita
Γλυκιά Κολοκυθόπιτα

MAKES: 24 PIECES
TIME: 2 HOURS

½ cup sultanas

½ cup freshly squeezed orange juice

700 g (24.6 oz. /1.5 lb.) grated butternut pumpkin

½ cup walnuts, crushed

4 tablespoons almond meal

1 cup castor (superfine) sugar

3 tablespoons sesame seeds

1½ teaspoons ground cloves

1½ teaspoons ground nutmeg

2 tablespoons cinnamon powder

500 g (17.6 oz. /1.1 lb.) filo pastry

¾ cup olive oil

Preheat the oven to 190°C (374°F).

Place the sultanas, orange juice, pumpkin, walnuts, almond meal, sugar, sesame, and spices in a bowl. Mix together well. Pour this mixture into a sieve with a bowl underneath to catch the juices from the moisture of the pumpkin and the orange juice. Allow this to stand 10 minutes, and then squeeze the mixture with your hands to further release any juice. Reserve the juices.

Oil a baking dish that is approximately 32 cm long, 25 cm wide, and 6 cm deep (12 in. by 9 in. by 2 in.).

Set aside 10 sheets of filo pastry covered with a damp cloth. These will be used for the top layers.

Using the remaining filo pastry, start to layer the sheets into the baking dish, oiling each layer as you go. Start with 5 sheets and place approximately ¼ of the pumpkin mixture on top. Repeat this process until you have used all the mixture. Gently press the layers down with your hands to create a nice, flat surface before placing on the last 10 top layers, ensuring that each filo is brushed with oil. Score the pastry into diamond shapes with a sharp knife. Take the reserved juices and pour them over the pie.

Bake the pie for 1 hour or until it is golden.

Serve this pie warm or cold with vanilla ice cream and a dusting of icing (confectioner's) sugar.

My mother and my sister are the lemon lovers in my family; they would slice lemon wedges, dip them in sugar, and indulge in that sour squirt. Somehow, though, I find myself thinking of my husband and brother-in-law, Savvas, when this cake comes to mind. They both love yogurt, and they both like cake, so it makes sense that this one is a winner with them. Greek strained yogurt is so versatile, and using it in cakes demonstrates how moist the results can be. Lemons are plentiful, and olive oil is always in abundance. This is a traditional, pleasant, fragrant cake that is best made a day or two in advance.

Yogurt-Olive Oil Sponge Cake

Giaourtopita Me Eleolado
Γιαουρτόπιτα Με Ελαιόλαδο

MAKES: 15 PIECES
PREP: 20 MINUTES
BAKING: 40 MINUTES

6 eggs, separated

1 cup light olive oil

1½ cups castor (superfine) sugar

Zest of 2 lemons

Zest of ½ an orange

1½ cups Greek yogurt

3 cups all-purpose flour

3 teaspoons baking powder

Icing (confectioner's) sugar, for dusting

Preheat the oven to 190°C (374°F).

Grease a 26 cm diameter (10 in.) ring tin with oil, and then flour it.

Whisk the egg whites until they form soft peaks. Set them aside.

Beat the oil and sugar until they are combined. Add the egg yolks gradually, and then add the lemon zest, orange zest, and yogurt. Mix everything until it is well combined, and then slowly add the flour and baking powder. Once the ingredients are combined, fold in the egg whites until the ingredients are just combined, being careful not to over mix.

Pour the cake batter into the ring tin and bake for 45 minutes or until a skewer inserted comes out clean. Unmold the cake immediately. Dust it with a liberal sprinkling of icing sugar. Allow it to cool before cutting. It's best eaten a day later and stays fresh for up to 4 days.

Engagingly attractive, these little croissant-shaped pastries appeal not only to the eyes but also to the palate. This dessert is a crumbly, tasty pastry made with olive oil and Turkish delight. While they are still hot from the oven, the pastries are treated with a brushing of rose water, which then seeps into the pastry and gives them a subtle extra sweetness. I love the fact that there is little sugar in the pastry—it is a great treat.

Olive Oil Pastries Stuffed with Turkish Delights

Gemista Stroufihta me Eleolado kai Loukoumi
Γεμιστά Στρουφιχτά με Ελαιόλαδο και Λουκούμι

MAKES: 40 PIECES
TIME: 1 HOUR, 15 MINUTES

- 1 cup light olive oil
- 2 eggs
- ½ cup castor (superfine) sugar
- 300 mL (10 fl. oz.) thickened cream (heavy cream)
- 4–5 cups all-purpose flour
- 20 pieces of Turkish delight,* cut in half
- 2 cups icing (confectioner's) sugar to dust
- ½ cup rose water*

Preheat the oven to 190°C (374°F).

In a mixer, beat the olive oil, eggs, and sugar for 2–3 minutes.

Gradually add the cream to the egg mixture and mix on medium speed for another 3 minutes, making sure the cream does not whip and thicken. Add the flour 1 cup at a time until you have a soft but not sticky dough. The dough will start to come away from the bowl when it's ready.

Separate the dough into 6 equal pieces. Place 1 piece between 2 pieces of parchment paper. Using a rolling pin, roll the dough into a circular base approximately 23 cm (9 in.) in diameter and roughly 0.5 cm (5 mm) thick.

Divide the base into 8 pieces the same way you would cut a pizza. Take 1 piece of Turkish delight, and place it along the outer edge of each piece. Roll each piece toward the center of the base to create a croissant shape.

Place the pastries on a lined baking tray. Bake them approximately 25 minutes or until they are light golden brown. Remove them from the oven and immediately brush them with rose water.

Allow the pastries to cool slightly, and then dust them with icing sugar. They stay fresh for up to 1 week.

—

Both rose water and Turkish delights are sold at international delicatessens.

Spoon sweets are everywhere in Greece, and the varieties are endless. Made from anything from baby eggplants to pistachios, these preserves always taste amazing. No doubt every Greek home has a jar somewhere in its pantry. They are called spoon sweets because they are served on small plates and with small spoons. They are intensely sweet, so one spoonful is usually enough to satisfy. They are served with a Greek coffee or a glass of cold water. It is a welcoming, hospitable gesture to be given spoon sweets when you enter a Greek home. Spoon sweets are delicious spooned over Greek yogurt.

Grape Spoon Sweet

Gliko tou Koutaliou

Γλυκό του Κουταλιού

GLUTEN-FREE
MAKES: 1 LARGE JAR
PREP: 10 MINUTES
COOKING:
4-5 HOURS

Wash the grapes and remove the stems.

In a saucepan, combine the grapes and sugar. Let them stand for 2 hours.

Place the grape mixture on the stove over medium to high heat until it starts to froth and boil. With a spoon, remove as much froth as possible. Lower the heat and simmer the mixture, uncovered, for approximately 2–3 hours.

To check if it is ready, taste a grape—it should be soft, and the syrup should be like glucose in consistency.

Place 1 spoonful on a cold plate, and if the syrup does not run off quickly, it is ready.

Remove the spoon sweet from the stove. Add the lemon juice and almonds. Mix the ingredients together. Allow the spoon sweet to cool, and then pour into a jar. Keep the spoon sweets refrigerated for up to a month.

1 kg (35.2 oz. / 2.2 lb.) seedless grapes

810 g (28.5 oz. / 1.7 lb.) castor (superfine) sugar

1½ tablespoons lemon juice

½ cup slivered almonds

Greek coffee plays a major role in the lives of Greeks. Beans are roasted medium to dark, ground to a very fine powder, and then slowly brewed to create a unique taste. In every home, you will find various sizes of *brikia*, the pot used to brew the coffee. From small to large, these pots are always in sight. Whether you have a cup for breakfast, lunch, or supper (or many more times throughout the day), coffee is essential. It brings people together, primarily in the *kafenia* in Greece. Kafenia are coffee shops where the men generally pass their time (the women go to sweet shops for coffee). Here, men play backgammon, twist their *komboloi* (similar to a worry bead but called a "pastime"), and catch up with each other's news. Hours and hours are spent here while the men slurp away at their coffee.

Greek coffee is to be made slowly and deliberately drunk leisurely. Taking small, loud sips enhances the experience and expresses a delight in the coffee. There is sediment of the coffee (at the bottom of the cup) that should not be drunk. Greek coffee is always served with a glass of cold water.

Greek coffee is made on the stove and is traditionally served in white espresso-size cups.

The *crema* on the top of the coffee is a very important sign that the coffee is made well. My grandmother would say to me, "When you can get a nice layer of *kaimaki* [*crema*], you are ready for marriage!" So, to ensure a good *crema*, the coffee must be brewed very slowly.

Greek Coffee

Ellinikos Kafes
Ελληνικός Καφές

Δεν είναι
κακό να είσαι
μέτριος...αρκεί
να είσαι καφές.

There are three main ways you can enjoy Greek coffee. If you like a sweeter coffee, you can add more sugar.

When ordering coffee, you ask for one of these three styles:

Sketos: no sugar and one teaspoon of coffee
Glikos: sweet: one teaspoon of coffee and two teaspoons of sugar
Metrios: slightly sweet: one teaspoon of coffee and one teaspoon of sugar

HOW TO PREPARE:
Fill the cup to the top with water. Pour it into the briki and add 1 teaspoon of coffee and sugar, depending on the option you choose from the above 3 styles. Place this mixture on the stove top over medium to low heat. Stir to dissolve the sugar and coffee and allow the coffee to gradually come to a slow boil. As soon as it slowly starts to rise, turn off the heat and slowly pour it into the cup in a steady stream. There should be a shiny but thin stream of crema on the top. Serve Greek coffee with a glass of cold water. Remember: drink slowly, but take loud sips. Enjoy!

Index

Items marked with GF indicate gluten-free.

A

ALMONDS

Almond and Orange Shortbreads	224
Grape Spoon Sweet GF	241
Greek Biscotti with Orange and Honey	213
Hot Cheese Dip GF	70
Olive Oil Cake with Orange Blossom Syrup	196-197
Orange-Apricot Semolina Pudding	204
Sesame, Salted Pistachio, and Rose Water Baklava	198-199
Sweet Easter Bread	206-207

APPETIZERS

Cauliflower with Feta Cheese	84
Eggplant Dip GF	72
Greek Bruschetta	78
Hot Cheese Dip GF	70
Olives GF	75
Pickled Octopus GF	62
Pork, Fennel, and Orange Sausages GF	82
Skordalia GF	71
Stuffed Baby Peppers GF	60
Tzatziki GF	65
Yogurt Pastry Miniature Cheese Pies	81

APPLES

Capsicum and Apple Salsa GF	98

APRICOTS

Orange-Apricot Semolina Pudding	204

B

Baked Snapper	184

BAKLAVA

Sesame, Salted Pistachio, and Rose Water Baklava	198-199

BEANS

Bean Soup GF	112
Lima Beans Two Ways GF	176
Long Green Bean Stew with Olive Oil GF	104

BEEF

Cabbage Rolls with Lemon GF	120-121
Cumin Meatballs GF	163
Egg Meat Loaf	172-173
Kephalonian Beef Stew	111
Little Eggplant Shoes GF	146-147
Meatball and Rice Soup GF	100
Moussaka GF	174-175
Pastitsio	158-159

BELL PEPPER(S) (Capsicum)

Stuffed Baby Peppers GF	60
Capsicum and Apple Salsa GF	98
Eggplant Dip GF	72
Greek Bruschetta	78
Greek Salad GF	64
Hot Cheese Dip GF	70
Little Eggplant Shoes GF	146-147
Long Green Bean Stew with Olive Oil GF	104
Roasted Capsicum Salad	90
Vegetable Bake GF	155
Vegetarian Moussaka GF	144-145

BISCOTTI

Greek Biscotti with Orange and Honey	213

BISCUITS

Prune-Stuffed, Honey-Soaked Biscuits	220

BREAD(S)
- Flatbreads — 118
- Olive Oil and Feta Bread — 160
- Sesame and Fennel Seed — 76
- Sweet Easter Bread — 206-207

BRUSCHETTA
- Greek Bruschetta — 78

C

Cabbage Rolls with Lemon GF — 120-121

CAKES
- Olive Oil Cake with Orange Blossom Syrup — 196-197
- Yogurt-Olive Oil Sponge Cake — 237

CAPERS
- Greek Salad GF — 64
- Lemon-Dressed Potato Salad — 124

CAPSICUM (Bell pepper)
- Capsicum and Apple Salsa GF — 98
- Eggplant Dip GF — 72
- Hot Cheese Dip GF — 70
- Long Green Bean Stew with Olive Oil GF — 104
- Roasted Capsicum Salad — 90
- Vegetable Bake GF — 155
- Vegetarian Moussaka GF — 144-145

Cauliflower with Feta Cheese — 84

CHEESE. *See also specific cheeses*
- Hot Cheese Dip GF — 70
- Cheese Pie — 141
- Lazy Housewife Cheese Pie — 179
- Yogurt Pastry Miniature Cheese Pies — 81

CHEESECAKE
- Greek Yogurt Cheesecake with Ouzo Poached Figs — 230-231

CHICKEN
- Cinnamon Chicken with Lemon Potatoes GF — 103
- Chicken and Rice Soup GF — 106

Chickpea Soup GF — 99

CHOCOLATE
- Ouzo Cookies with Jam — 214-215

CINNAMON
- Capsicum and Apple Salsa GF — 98
- Cinnamon Chicken with Lemon Potatoes GF — 103
- Flatbreads — 118
- Greek Biscotti with Orange and Honey — 213
- Greek Yogurt Cheesecake with Ouzo Poached Figs — 230-231
- Honey Donuts — 229
- Kephalonian Beef Stew — 111
- Long Green Bean Stew with Olive Oil GF — 104
- Mastiha Pudding — 218-219
- Milk Pie — 192-193
- Moussaka GF — 174-175
- Okra with Lamb and Potatoes GF — 150
- Olive Oil Cake with Orange Blossom Syrup — 196-197
- Orange-Apricot Semolina Pudding — 204
- Orange-Scented Rice Pudding GF — 223
- Pastitsio — 158-159
- Prune-Stuffed, Honey-Soaked Biscuits — 220
- Rabbit and Onion Stew GF — 114
- Sesame and Nut Bars GF — 203
- Sesame, Salted Pistachio, and Rose Water Baklava — 198-199
- Squid with Orzo — 164
- Sweet Pumpkin Pie — 234

COFFEE
- Greek Coffee — 243
- Coiled Spinach Pie — 143

COOKIES
- Ouzo Cookies with Jam — 214-215

CUCUMBER(S)
- Greek Salad GF — 64
- Tzatziki GF — 65

Cumin Meatballs GF — 163

D

DESSERTS
- Almond and Orange Shortbreads — 224
- Grape Spoon Sweets GF — 241
- Greek Biscotti with Orange and Honey — 213
- Greek Yogurt Cheesecake with Ouzo Poached Figs — 230-231
- Honey Donuts — 229
- Mastiha Pudding — 218-219
- Milk Pie — 192-193
- Olive Oil Cake with Orange Blossom Syrup — 196-197
- Olive Oil Pastries Stuffed with Turkish Delight — 238
- Orange-Apricot Semolina Pudding — 204
- Orange-Scented Rice Pudding GF — 223
- Ouzo Cookies with Jam — 214-215
- Prune-Stuffed, Honey-Soaked Biscuits — 220
- Scrunched-Up Lemon Yogurt Pie — 210
- Sesame and Nut Bars GF — 203
- Sesame, Salted Pistachio, and Rose Water Baklava — 198-199
- Sweet Easter Bread — 206-207
- Sweet Pumpkin Pie — 234
- Yogurt-Olive Oil Sponge Cake — 237

Dolmadakia GF — 97

DONUTS
- Honey Donuts — 229

E

EGG(S)
- Egg Meat Loaf — 172-173
- Olive Oil Fried Potatoes with Egg and Feta Cheese GF — 94
- Peloponnese Red Eggs GF — 91
- Sweet Easter Bread — 206-207

EGGPLANT
- Eggplant Dip GF — 72
- Eggplant, Sausage, and Cream Rolls GF — 117
- Little Eggplant Shoes GF — 146-147
- Moussaka GF — 174-175
- Vegetable Bake GF — 155
- Vegetarian Moussaka GF — 144-145

F

FENNEL (SEED)
- Pork, Fennel, and Orange Sausages GF — 82
- Sesame and Fennel Seed Bread — 76

FETA CHEESE
- Cauliflower with Feta Cheese — 84
- Eggplant Dip GF — 72
- Flatbreads — 118
- Greek Bruschetta — 78
- Greek Salad GF — 64
- Hot Cheese Dip GF — 70
- Lazy Housewife Cheese Pie — 179

FETA CHEESE (cont.)
- Olive Oil and Feta Bread — 160
- Olive Oil Fried Potatoes with Egg and Feta Cheese GF — 94
- Ricotta Cheese Pie — 166
- Roasted Capsicum Salad — 90
- Stuffed Baby Peppers GF — 60
- Vegetarian Moussaka GF — 144-145
- Yogurt Pastry Miniature Cheese Pies — 81

FIGS
- Greek Yogurt Cheesecake Ouzo Poached Figs — 230-231

FISH. *See also* Snapper; Whitebait

Flatbreads — 118

Fried Whitebait GF — 109

G

GOAT
- Roasted Baby Goat with Potatoes GF — 154

Grape Spoon Sweet GF — 241

Greek Biscotti with Orange and Honey — 213

Greek Bruschetta — 78

Greek Coffee — 243

Greek Salad GF — 64

H

Homemade Filo Pastry — 140

Homemade Yogurt GF — 67

HONEY
- Honey Donuts — 229
- Greek Biscotti with Orange and Honey — 213
- Prune-Stuffed Honey-Soaked Biscuits — 220

Hot Cheese Dip GF — 70

K

KEFALOGRAVIERA CHEESE
- Cauliflower with Feta Cheese — 84
- Eggplant, Sausage, and Cream Rolls GF — 117
- Little Eggplant Shoes GF — 146-147
- Moussaka GF — 174-175
- Pastitsio — 158-159

KEFALOTIRI CHEESE
- Vegetarian Moussaka GF — 144-145

Kephalonian Beef Stew — 111

L

LAMB
- Cumin Meatballs GF — 163
- Moussaka GF — 174-175
- Okra with Lamb and Potatoes GF — 150
- Roasted Lamb with Lemon Potatoes GF — 168

Lazy Housewife Cheese Pie, 179

LEMON(S)
- Cabbage Rolls with Lemon GF — 120-121
- Cinnamon Chicken with Lemon Potatoes GF — 103
- Lemon-Dressed Potato Salad — 124

LEMON(S) (cont.)
    Roasted Lamb with Lemon Potatoes GF   168
    Scrunched-Up Lemon Yogurt Pie   210

Lentil Soup GF   110

Lima Beans Two Ways GF   176

Little Eggplant Shoes GF   146-147

Long Green Bean Stew with Olive Oil GF   104

M

MAHLEPI
    Sweet Easter Bread   206-207

MASTIHA
    Mastiha Pudding   218-219

MASTIHA (cont.)
    Olive Oil Cake with Orange Blossom Syrup   196-197
    Sesame and Nut Bars GF   203
    Sweet Easter Bread   206-207

Meatball and Rice Soup GF   100

Milk Pie   192-193

MINT
    Cabbage Rolls with Lemon GF   120-121
    Cumin Meatballs GF   163
    Dolmadakia GF   97
    Egg Meat Loaf   172-173
    Little Eggplant Shoes GF   146-147
    Meatball and Rice Soup GF   100
    Roasted Capsicum Salad   90
    Spinach Pie   141
    Stuffed Baby Peppers GF   60

MINT (cont.)
    Stuffed Squid GF   180
    Stuffed Tomatoes GF   153
    Vegetable Bake GF   155
    Yogurt Pastry Miniature Cheese Pies   81

MIZITHRA
    Kephalonian Beef Stew   111

Moussaka GF   174-175

O

OCTOPUS
    Pickled Octopus GF   62

Okra with Lamb and Potatoes GF   150

OLIVE(S)
    Eggplant Dip GF   72
    Greek Bruschetta   78
    Greek Salad GF   64
    Lemon-Dressed Potato Salad   124

Olives GF   75

OLIVE OIL
    Long Green Bean Stew with Olive Oil GF   104
    Olive Oil Cake with Orange Blossom Syrup   196-197
    Olive Oil and Feta Bread   160
    Olive Oil Fried Potatoes with Egg and Feta Cheese GF   94
    Olive Oil Pastries Stuffed with Turkish Delight   238
    Yogurt-Olive Oil Sponge Cake   237

ONION(S). *See also* Red onion(s)
    Rabbit and Onion Stew GF   114
    Vegetable Bake GF   155

ORANGE(S)

Almond and Orange Shortbreads	224
Greek Biscotti with Honey and Honey	213
Olive Oil Cake with Orange Blossom Syrup	196-197
Orange-Apricot Semolina Pudding	204
Orange-Scented Rice Pudding GF	223
Prune-Stuffed, Honey-Soaked Biscuits	220
Pork, Fennel, and Orange Sausages GF	82

ORZO

Squid with Orzo	164

OUZO

Greek Biscotti with Orange and Honey	213
Greek Yogurt Cheesecake with Ouzo Poached Figs	230-231
Ouzo Cookies with Jam	214-215

P

PARSLEY

Baked Snapper GF	184
Cabbage Rolls with Lemon GF	120-121
Cumin Meatballs GF	163
Dolmadakia GF	97
Egg Meat Loaf	172-173
Eggplant Dip GF	72
Greek Bruschetta	78
Lemon-Dressed Potato Salad	124
Lima Beans Two Ways GF	176
Little Eggplant Shoes GF	146-147
Meatball and Rice Soup GF	100
Roasted Capsicum Salad	90
Spinach Pie	141
Stuffed Squid GF	180
Stuffed Tomatoes GF	153

PARSLEY (cont.)

Vegetable Bake GF	155

Pastitsio 158-159

PASTRIES. *See also* Pie(s)

Homemade Filo	140
Mastiha Pudding	218-219
Olive Oil Pastries Stuffed with Turkish Delights	238
Sesame, Salted Pistachio, and Rose Water Baklava	198-199
Yogurt Pastry Miniature Cheese Pies	81

PEANUTS

Ouzo Cookies with Jam GF	214-215

Peloponnese Red Eggs GF 91

PEPPERS. *See* Bell pepper(s); Capsicum

Stuffed Baby Peppers GF	60

Pickled Octopus GF 62 GF

PIES

Cheese Pie	141
Coiled Spinach Pie	143
Lazy Housewife Cheese Pie	179
Milk Pie	192-193
Ricotta Cheese Pie	166
Savory Pumpkin Pie	141
Scrunched-Up Lemon Yogurt Pie	210
Spinach Pie	141
Sweet Pumpkin Pie	234
Yogurt Pastry Miniature Cheese Pie	81

PISTACHIO(S)

Sesame and Nut Bars GF	203
Sesame, Salted Pistachio, and Rose Water Baklava	198-199

PORK
- Cabbage Rolls with Lemon GF — 120-121
- Eggplant, Sausage, and Cream Rolls GF — 117
- Pork, Fennel, and Orange Sausages GF — 82

POTATO(ES)
- Baked Snapper GF — 184
- Bean Soup GF — 112
- Cinnamon Chicken with Lemon Potatoes GF — 103
- Lemon-Dressed Potato Salad — 124
- Long Green Bean Stew with Olive Oil GF — 104
- Moussaka GF — 174-175
- Okra with Lamb and Potatoes GF — 150
- Olive Oil Fried Potatoes with Egg and Feta Cheese GF — 94
- Roasted Baby Goat with Potatoes GF — 154
- Roasted Lamb with Lemon Potatoes GF — 168
- Skordalia GF — 71
- Vegetable Bake GF — 155
- Vegetarian Moussaka GF — 144-145

PROSCIUTTO
- Egg Meat Loaf — 172-173

PUDDINGS
- Mastiha Pudding — 218-219
- Orange-Apricot Semolina Pudding — 204
- Orange-Scented Rice Pudding GF — 223

PUMPKIN
- Bean Soup GF — 112
- Lima Beans Two Ways GF — 176
- Long Green Bean Stew with Olive Oil GF — 104
- Savory Pumpkin — 141
- Sweet Pumpkin Pie — 234

Prune-Stuffed, Honey-Soaked Biscuits — 220

R

Rabbit and Onion Stew GF — 114

RED ONION(S)
- Greek Bruschetta — 78
- Greek Salad GF — 64

RICE
- Cabbage Rolls with Lemon GF — 120-121
- Chicken and Rice Soup GF — 106
- Dolmadakia GF — 97
- Meatball and Rice Soup GF — 100
- Orange-Scented Rice Pudding GF — 223
- Stuffed Squid GF — 180
- Stuffed Tomatoes GF — 153

RICOTTA
- Ricotta Cheese Pie — 166
- Yogurt Pastry Miniature Cheese Pies — 81

Roasted Baby Goat with Potatoes GF — 154

Roasted Capsicum (Bell Pepper) Salad — 90

Roasted Lamb with Lemon Potatoes GF — 168

ROSE WATER
- Greek Yogurt Cheesecake with Ouzo Poached Figs — 230-231
- Olive Oil Pastries Stuffed with Turkish Delight — 238
- Sesame, Salted Pistachio, and Rose Water Baklava — 198-199

S

SALADS
- Greek Salad GF — 64
- Lemon-Dressed Potato Salad — 124
- Roasted Capsicum (Bell Pepper) Salad — 90

Savory Pumpkin Pie — 41

Scrunched-Up Lemon Yogurt Pie — 210

SEAFOOD
- Baked Snapper GF — 184
- Fried Whitebait GF — 109
- Pickled Octopus GF — 62
- Squid with Orzo — 164
- Stuffed Squid GF — 180

SEMOLINA
- Orange-Apricot Semolina Pudding — 204

SESAME (SEEDS)
- Sesame and Fennel Seed Bread — 76
- Sesame and Nut Bars GF — 203
- Sesame, Salted Pistachio, and Rose Water Baklava — 198-199

SHORTBREADS
- Almond and Orange Shortbreads — 224

Skordalia GF — 71

SNAPPER
- Baked Snapper GF — 184

SOUPS
- Bean Soup GF — 112
- Chicken and Rice Soup GF — 106
- Chickpea Soup GF — 99

SOUPS (cont.)
- Lentil Soup GF — 110
- Meatball and Rice Soup GF — 100

SPAGHETTI
- Pastitsio — 158-159

SPINACH
- Spinach Pie — 141
- Coiled Spinach Pie — 143

SPOON SWEETS
- Grape Spoon Sweet GF — 241

SQUID
- Squid with Orzo — 164
- Stuffed Squid GF — 180

STEWS
- Kephalonian Beef Stew — 111
- Long Green Bean Stew with Olive Oil GF — 104
- Rabbit and Onion Stew GF — 114

Stuffed Baby Peppers GF — 60

Stuffed Squid GF — 180

Stuffed Tomatoes GF — 153

Sweet Easter Bread — 206-207

Sweet Pumpkin Pie — 234

T

TOMATO(ES)
- Capsicum and Apple Salsa GF — 98
- Greek Bruschetta — 78
- Greek Salad GF — 64

TOMATO(ES) (cont.)

Long Green Bean Stew with Olive Oil GF	104
Peloponnese Red Eggs GF	91
Roasted Baby Goat with Potatoes GF	154
Stuffed Tomatoes GF	153

TURKISH DELIGHTS

Olive Oil Pastries Stuffed with Turkish Delights	238

Tzatziki GF 65

V

Vegetable Bake GF 155

Vegetarian Moussaka GF 144-145

VINE LEAVES

Dolmadakia GF	97

W

WALNUTS

Prune-Stuffed, Honey-Soaked Biscuits	220
Sesame, Salted Pistachio, and Rose Water Baklava	198-199
Sweet Pumpkin Pie	234

WHITEBAIT

Fried Whitebait GF	109

Y

YOGURT

Cabbage Rolls with Lemon GF	120-121
Dolmadakia GF	97
Greek Yogurt Cheesecake with Ouzo Poached Figs	230-231
Homemade Yogurt GF	67
Scrunched-Up Lemon Yogurt Pie	210
Tzatziki GF	65
Yogurt-Olive Oil Sponge Cake	237
Yogurt Pastry Miniature Cheese Pies	81

Z

ZUCCHINI(S)

Vegetable Bake	155
Vegetarian Moussaka	144-145

Acknowledgments

It's hard to note all the individuals who assisted in making this book a reality. It has very definitely been a combined effort. My great passion for cooking and my enjoyment of seeing others eating what I set before them are no doubt some of the reasons this book now exists. So, thank you to every person who has eaten anything I made—you may not have known it, but I was seriously noting your comments, your support, and your confidence in my venture, and on account of that, I decided to bring this book to fruition.

To my parents, Jim and Paula: Dad, thank you for the inspiration to reach for the stars and for the support you gave me, trusting that I could do this and do it well. Mum, thank you for planting seeds of joy in your homemaking, inevitably inspiring me to do the same and better still.

Thanks to my in-laws, who brought even more love into my life. I am truly blessed with you.

Thanks to my siblings, brothers-in-law, sister-in-law, nieces, and nephews, who tasted and wanted recipes that I promised would be in this book. Here you have it, to keep and to share with your families.

Matthew Pilarinos, thank you for the continual critiquing, photo after photo. Thank you for encouraging me to push further. Thank you for loving food as much as I do—it's a joy to cook for you.

Much appreciation to my grandmother Angela, who, though she is not with us now, needs a prominent mention—my culinary roots start with her!

Thank you to my many uncles and aunties, whom I have watched and who have shared family recipes with me.

I send my gratitude to my precious friends in Greece, Australia, and America, who ate and gave me so much feedback as I tested and photographed each meal.

Thank you, Larry and Kathleen Hausman, for the use of your home to photograph some meals; to Lucas and Indira Almeida for the amazing sausages we made together and that were used for this book; to Hannah Carter for the unintentional, but great photograph on page 256; to Wesley Parsons, who has probably eaten the most in my kitchen as I undertook this project—thank you all.

Thanks to those in Greece who shared knowledge and graciously assisted me. Thank you, Myrtia Fragopoulou, for being my Greek spelling checker. Thank you to my editors and my publisher and graphic designer, Sara Ekart.

To Athanasios, thank you for loving me and for being patient as you watched me advance word by word, recipe by recipe, trying and testing each meal. Thank you for being there and making this project a joint effort of love. Thank you for spurring me to complete this, and thank you for being deliberate in eating every meal together and making the family table such a joy. I love you and want this to always be true for us: *"How beautiful is your love, my sister, my bride! How much better is your love than wine, and the fragrance of your oils than any spice!" (Song of Solomon 4:10)*.